Secrets of the Freemasons

PUBLISHER'S NOTE

The views expressed herein are the personal views of the author and
are not intended to reflect the views of the publisher.

STERLING and the distinctive Sterling logo are registered trademarks of
Sterling Publishing Co., Inc.

Library of Congress Cataloging-in-Publication Data Available

4 6 8 10 9 7 5

Published by Sterling Publishing Co., Inc.
387 Park Avenue South, New York, NY 10016
© 2006 by Fall River Press / Sterling Publishing Co., Inc.
Distributed in Canada by Sterling Publishing
ᶜ/o Canadian Manda Group, 165 Dufferin Street
Toronto, Ontario, Canada M6K 3H6

Photo and illustration credits appear on page 207.
Book design by Allen Boe

Printed in China
All rights reserved

Sterling ISBN 978-1-4027-6316-8

For information about custom editions, special sales, premium and
corporate purchases, please contact Sterling Special Sales
Department at 800-805-5489 or specialsales@sterlingpublishing.com.

Secrets of the Freemasons

Michael Bradley

STERLING

New York / London

www.sterlingpublishing.com

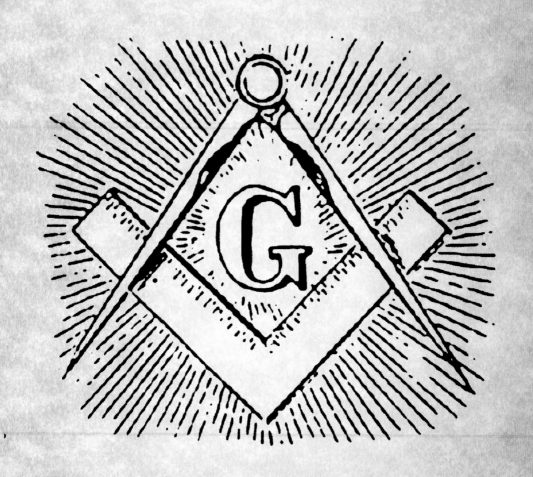

Contents

Introduction

During the last three hundred years, thousands of books, pamphlets, and manuscripts have been written about Freemasonry. Many of them have been penned by Freemasons attempting to add their interpretations of the great truths hidden within its labyrinthine symbolic system, to expand on already impenetrable and over-subscribed legends, or merely to self-promote.

At the other end of the spectrum there are numerous books by non-Masons that attempt to expose Masonic secrets, and demonstrate how this powerful organization has been covertly directing world events since pre-Christian times. Those books take the reader on a tantalizing journey, mixing speculation with historical analysis, and they often pose more questions than they answer. This book falls into the latter category, but unlike many of its kind, it avoids speculation and spurious conspiracies. Nevertheless, it still succeeds in presenting an image of the Craft that is greatly at odds with its public face.

As Michael Baigent and Richard Leigh point out in *The Temple and the Lodge*, Freemasons "have often sought a single coherent heritage, a single skein of tradition extending from pre-Christian times to the present day. In fact, Freemasonry is rather like a ball of twine ensnarled by a playful kitten. It consists of numerous skeins, which must be disentangled before its various origins can be discerned."

This implies that a single narrative exists. In fact, exploring the murky depths of Freemasonry is more like attempting to salvage an old shipwreck buried on the ocean floor and inside a hall of mirrors. At every turn there are exciting discoveries, many of which are illusions; the more one digs around, the worse the visibility becomes, as the accumulated detritus of previous generations, scholars, apologists, occultists, and conspiracy theorists clouds the view.

Masonry has thrived through this disinformation coupled with its ability to attract aristocratic and influential members of society. Its ranks boast some of the greatest thinkers, artists, businessmen, and leaders of the last four centuries.

America's first president, George Washington, was a Mason. Several of the Founding Fathers were Masons, including Ethan Allen, John Paul Jones, Paul Revere, John Hancock, and Benjamin Franklin. Of the fifty-six signatories to the Declaration of Independence, eight admitted to being Freemasons, along with at least sixteen U.S. presidents: James Madison, James Monroe, Andrew Jackson, James Polk, James Buchanan, Andrew Johnson, James A. Garfield, William McKinley, Theodore Roosevelt, William Howard Taft, Warren G. Harding, Franklin D. Roosevelt, Harry S. Truman, Lyndon B. Johnson, Gerald Ford, and Ronald Reagan. In England, royalty has been involved in Freemasonry since its inception. Some members were openly Masonic; some left clues in their work, literature, music, or art; while others left scant evidence that they were part of the Brotherhood.

While this bounty hunting is as exciting as it is exhausting, any attempt to retrieve this large, cumbersome, and fragile artifact in one piece risks destroying the very thing one is trying to save, while shattering the revisionist and self-referential framework which surrounds it.

Similarly, trying to create a simple linear account is fruitless, since fact and fiction, myth and legend, are intrinsic building blocks of Freemasonry. Consequently, this book attempts to anchor its analysis of the Craft by shining a spotlight on several key historical and political events, exploring the darker side of Masonic conspiracies, murders, and world manipulation.

Gene Autry (1907–1998)

Initiated 1927, Catoosa Lodge No. 185, Oklahoma

The only entertainer to have five stars on Hollywood's Walk of Fame, with a career in entertainment spanning seventy years, the "Singing Cowboy" was a 33rd degree Mason and Honorary Inspector General and was awarded the prestigious Grand Cross of the Court of Honor. He was initiated in Catoosa Lodge No. 185, Catoosa, Oklahoma, in 1927. He became a Life Member of Long Beach, California (33rd degree A.A.S.R.), as well as a Life Member of Malaika Shrine Temple at Los Angeles, California.

 Famous Freemasons Past and Present

William "Count" Basie (1904–1984)

Initiated Wisdom Lodge No. 102, Chicago, Illinois

Basie was a leading figure of the swing era in jazz and a big band contemporary of Duke Ellington (another Mason). As a young man he came to New York and studied informally under Fats Waller, another pianist of the Harlem stride school and a Mason.

 Famous Freemasons Past and Present

Ludwig van Beethoven (1770–1827)

Lodge unconfirmed

In *Late Beethoven: Music, Thought, Imagination*, Maynard Solomon examines Beethoven's Masonic contacts and innumerable references to Masonic imagery and concludes that he was a Mason, even though his lodge membership details cannot be traced.

There is no definite proof that Beethoven was a Mason, but there are good grounds for believing he was. Many of his friends and fellow musicians were Masons, and there are several references to Masonry in his correspondence.

The hauntingly beautiful slow movement of his "String Quartet No. 7 in F major" bears the inscription, "A weeping willow or acacia tree on the grave of my brother" (Acacia is often placed in graves, or on coffins, at Masonic funerals as a symbol of the immortality of the soul). Both of Beethoven's brothers were alive when this was written, so it is most likely a Masonic reference. He also attended concerts at which full Masonic rites were observed. It seems unlikely that he would have been allowed to do this if he wasn't a Mason.

 Famous Freemasons Past and Present

Irving Berlin (1888–1989)

Initiated 1910, Munn Lodge No. 190, New York

Mason Jerome Kern famously said that "Irving Berlin has no place in American music—he is American music." He was a Mason for 79 years, receiving the 32nd degree A.A.S.R. (NJ) on December 23, 1910, and he was initiated into Mecca Shrine Temple on January 30, 1911. He wrote at least one song with overt Masonic connotations, called "Hiram's Band," written around 1912 in collaboration with E. Ray Goetz.

 Famous Freemasons Past and Present

Robert Burns (1759–1796)

Initiated 1781, Saint David's Lodge No. 2174, Tarbolton, Scotland

The farmer's son who became the Scottish national poet joined six lodges, the first of which was in 1781. Later, he became the master of a lodge in Mauchline. Burns wrote "The Farewell" when he was planning to immigrate to the West Indies to work on a sugar plantation.

> "May Freedom, Harmony, and Love,
> Unite you in the grand Design,
> Beneath th' Omniscient Eye above,
> The glorious Architect Divine . . ."
> "The Farewell," 1786

 Famous Freemasons Past and Present

Winston Churchill
(1874–1965)

Initiated 1901, Studholme Lodge, London (now Studholme Alliance Lodge No. 1591)

He was initiated at the age of twenty-six and appears to have been a regular attender, but he resigned in 1912 due to political commitments, and actually published his letter of resignation. He never rejoined, although in 1918 he was a petitioner for a new London Lodge, the Ministry of Munitions Lodge (Churchill was the Minister of Munitions at the time).

 Famous Freemasons Past and Present

Nat "King" Cole
(1919–1965)

Initiated Thomas Waller Lodge No. 49, Los Angeles, California PHA

The musical pioneer, jazz pianist, and pop singer Nathaniel Adams Coles was born in Montgomery, Alabama, and christened Nat "King" Cole by a Los Angeles club owner in 1937.

 Famous Freemasons Past and Present

CHAPTER 1
Early History

❦

Most historians agree that Freemasonry as we know it today developed from the guilds of medieval operative stonemasons who built the Gothic cathedrals of Europe.

The origin of the word "Freemason" has two possible interpretations. The first is that masons moved around from city to city, so they were "free" in the sense that they were mobile. The other is a shortening of the term "freestone mason." Freestone is a type of fine-grained stone which can be carved.

Centuries earlier, the Angles and Saxons settled in ancient Britain and established a military form of organization. A civil system of social order developed (guilds) alongside it, initially founded on blood ties (e.g., the clans of Scotland) and later on community ties.

The first guilds were organized in Italy, and commercial guilds became popular in France and Scandinavia as a means of suppressing piracy. Their scope grew so that by the thirteenth century guilds had become the outstanding feature of the social and economic life of Europe. There were guilds for everything: good-fellowship, drinking, covering burial expenses, hunting, travel, and every conceivable profession from woodsmen to swineherd. Men and women, rich and poor—all could belong, and did.

OPERATIVE, ACCEPTED, AND SPECULATIVE MASONRY

During the Middle Ages, the Masonic guilds consisted entirely of "operative" masons, that is, skilled laborers who worked with stone. Gradually, beginning in the sixteenth century, men who were not skilled craftsmen were "accepted" into the guilds. It was the Masonic equivalent of a modern-day university bestowing an honorary degree. By the eighteenth century, Masonry was almost exclusively "speculative," consisting of men from all walks of life, who speculated upon (in the sense that they interpreted) the symbols and artifacts of operative masonry. Where the operative Masons had built with stone, the speculative Masons aimed to construct spiritual, symbolic, and allegorical edifices.

There were very close links between guild and church. Pageantry, often with religious themes, was widespread. Mystery and morality plays, the forerunners of our modern dramas, were put on by the various guilds, each one presenting a different story. The elaborate dramas enacted by modern Freemasons *(see pages 54-67)* grew out of (or harken back to) these festival-day spectaculars, when plays were staged on wagons and drawn in procession through the streets. This tradition lives on today in the float processions of modern carnivals.

At the head of a typical guild were two or more wardens (a kind of medieval foreman who supervised the work performed by the craft and oversaw standards). The general membership was divided into three tiers: Masters, Fellow crafts (or journeymen), and Apprentices. (The same three names are used for the first three degrees of Blue Lodge Masonry today.) Women were admitted into many guilds and were permitted to take apprentices and hire fellow craft.

A youth became an apprentice and was "indentured" to a Master who would train him for an interval, fixed to seven years in 1563. The Master provided board and lodging and supervised the apprentice's conduct and training. The apprentice was expected to fulfill his commitments to be hard working, "no bondsman," and promote his master's welfare. After his training, and usually after he had created a "masterpiece" to showcase and demonstrate his skills, he would become a journeyman, and travel the country, or the world, to practice his craft and to consolidate his skills.

THE REGIUS MANUSCRIPT

Written at the end of the fourteenth century, this poem is the earliest known Masonic document. It lays out rules—fifteen of them—as well as a history tracing Freemasonry back to ancient Egypt. It instructs how a mason should conduct himself in business and in life.

Masons were in demand all over Europe during the Middle Ages, when Gothic churches were being built. In every major town and city there were Masonic lodges where a mason could get board, and find social and professional fellowship. Masons enjoyed an exalted position until the decline of Gothic architecture in the sixteenth century.

It is not known when the transition from Operative to Speculative Freemasonry occurred, but we do know that a Scottish Lodge was admitting non-operatives by 1672, and that some Lodges in England were completely Speculative by 1646.

SACRED GEOMETRY

Many occultists look back even further than the Middle Ages for the origins of Freemasonry. It is probable that the Masons gained their secret esoteric knowledge from a pagan hermetic tradition dating back to a pre-Christian era. It was this same knowledge—of sacred geometry—which enabled the Egyptians to build the great pyramids, and the Masons to build the Gothic churches of Europe.

The mythical origins of Freemasonry date back further still to the building of the Temple of King Solomon in Jerusalem around 1000 B.C. Stories and legends of King Solomon are found in the Old Testament (I Kings and II Chronicles) and subsequent Judaic and Islamic commentaries upon it.

HIRAM ABIFF

Freemasonry has elaborated on the Biblical story of the architect to such an extent that Hiram has become a figure of redemption and seems to represent a significant figure in theology. In the Masonic version, Hiram Abiff is in charge of the workers and is himself well versed in the secrets of geometry: number, shape, measure, and their application in construction. Because he cannot possibly know all the workers individually, the three degrees of workers are given their own word when it comes to collecting their wages. Apprentices are given the word "Boaz," Fellows the word "Jachin," and Masters the word "Jehovah." These important words appear in Masonic rituals (see pages 54–67).

However, Hiram is murdered by three villains who want to progress beyond their degree. He is struck on the head three times with a maul, or hammer; he is hit on one temple with a Level and on the other with a Plumb. The villains bury his body, and the Master Masons decide to devise a new word in case the word "Jehovah" has been divulged to the villains.

After discovering Hiram's body, they agree that the new word
will be whatever any of them should chance to utter as they are
lifting his body. One of the Masters said the word "Macbenae"
(which means "The flesh falls from the bone"; this appears as
"Ma-ha-bone" in the third degree ritual—see pages 64-65).
This becomes the new word. Hiram is buried in a ceremony
while all the other Masters wear their white gloves and aprons
to show that none of them are stained with his blood.

The Bible describes the building of the temple in great detail, including dimensions and measurement of various parts of the edifice. It says that Solomon conscripted workers from throughout Israel, 30,000 men in all, and sent them to Lebanon in shifts of 10,000 men per month. Solomon also had "70,000 common laborers and 80,000 stonemasons in the hills besides 3,300 officials who supervised the workers." The temple they built is the same three-tiered structure adopted by the Masons for the first three degrees of Masonry (*see page 30*). The supervisor of the crews was "Adoniram," which Baigent and Leigh claim is a variant spelling of Hiram, a key figure in Freemason mythology.

According to Masonic tradition, geometry had also been the sacred knowledge of a Enoch, a ruler who was instructed by an angel to preserve the secrets of civilization when the great flood was imminent. He did this by building an underground temple and hiding the geometrical knowledge within the dimensions of the building. In other words, the temple was itself an incarnation of the sacred secrets.

As Graham Hancock explains in *The Sign and the Seal*, ". . . The Book of Enoch has always been of great significance to Freemasons, and . . . certain rituals . . . identified Enoch himself with Thoth, the Egyptian god of wisdom."

Bear this in mind as you read on, because this tradition of encoding knowledge informs Masonic symbolism everywhere, from spelling out a demonic goathead pentagram on a dollar bill (*see page 145*) to the layout of a Masonic Lodge (*see page 27*).

THE GRAND LODGE AND THE BEGINNING OF SPECULATIVE MASONRY

The key date in the formation of modern Masonry is 1717. In June of this year, members of four Masonic lodges in London began meeting at the Goose and Gridiron Tavern, establishing the Grand Lodge of London and Westminster, which later became known as the Grand Lodge of England.

Modern Freemasonry was born during a time of immense social and technological change. There was a feeling in the air that great minds could come together to create a bright future, but at the same time day-to-day living conditions in England and America were grim, and a far cry from what we take for granted today.

Above: Title page of the Freemason Constitution

Early eighteenth-century London was a city without sewers, where the streets were filled with human and animal waste. The industrial revolution had not yet started. Science and philosophy were indistinguishable, and superstition was rampant (the last execution for witchcraft in England had taken place in 1712). But religion and its dogma, which had dominated every aspect of life during the Middle Ages, was beginning to be questioned as elite bodies of intellectuals led the world away from the long period of irrationality, superstition, and tyranny which had cast the long shadow of the Dark Ages. Many of these men joined Freemasonry and helped to usher in the Age of Reason.

The first meeting of the Grand Lodge didn't take place in a grand building. It was convened in the back room of a public house. Taverns were the focal point of social life, where people met to conduct business, eat, drink, and sing.

The elaborate Masonic symbolism *(see pages 38-49)* and initiation ceremonies *(see pages 54-67)* hadn't been invented yet. It seems, from the little we know from lodges of that period, that ceremonies were basic and brief, symbols were limited to the lodge panel, and there was no special furniture or physical tools. Symbols were drawn on a tracing board, or on the floor with chalk and coal, and then erased at the end of the meeting.

Masonic meetings were primarily social events, involving dinner, drinking, and, most important, singing. The Masonic lodges in these early days were not steeped in the ritual and symbolism which developed during the next few centuries. Men came together for conviviality and social refuge at a time of political and social uncertainty, when new scientific and economic opportunities were being developed, and when rationalism was beginning to lay the foundations for the humanistic and empirical society which we enjoy today. This was the cornerstone from which Freemasonry expanded to become a formalized and elitist club that eventually spread throughout the western world. The first Masonic Lodge opened in the United States on April 13, 1733, and grew rapidly. Today, of the six million Freemasons worldwide, about half are in the U.S.A.

Above: Mason Lord Allerton in Freemason costume

Initiation at a Freemason lodge

Cecil B. Demille
(1881–1959)
Initiated Prince of Orange Lodge No. 16, New York

The legendary film director and producer of epic extravaganzas *The Ten Commandments* and *The Greatest Show on Earth* is credited with being "the founder of Hollywood."

Famous Freemasons Past and Present

Edward Kennedy "Duke" Ellington
(1899–1974)
Initiated 1932, Social Lodge No. 1 DC, PHA

The American jazz composer, orchestrator, bandleader, and pianist is considered by many to be the greatest composer in the history of jazz music and one of the greatest musicians of the twentieth century.

Famous Freemasons Past and Present

Douglas Fairbanks Sr.
(1883–1939)

Initiated Beverly Hills Lodge No. 528, California

The son of a prominent Jewish attorney, the silent film actor is best known for his performance in swashbuckling adventures such as *Robin Hood*.

 Famous Freemasons Past and Present

Sir Alexander Fleming
(1881–1955)

Initiated 1909, Sancta Maria Lodge No. 2682, London

The farmer's son from Ayrshire in Scotland, who discovered penicillin in 1928, was a mason who was actually buried in St. Paul's Cathedral.

 Famous Freemasons Past and Present

Gerald Ford (1913–2006)

Initiated 1949, Malta Lodge No. 465,
Grand Rapids, Michigan

The thirty-eighth president of the United States was initiated in 1949 and was raised to Master Mason two years later. In 1962, he was made a Sovereign Grand Inspector General, 33rd degree, and Honorary Member, Supreme Council A.A.S.R. Northern Jurisdiction at the Academy of Music in Philadelphia. He was also an active member of the International Supreme Council, Order of DeMolay and its Honorary Grand Master from 1975 to 1977.

 Famous Freemasons Past and Present

Henry Ford (1863–1947)

Initiated 1894, Palestine Lodge No. 357,
Detroit, Michigan

Ford, the son of a prosperous farmer, grew up to revolutionize the automotive industry and factory mass production. He invented the automobile that changed the world. However, his life was not lived in accordance with Masonic principles as Neil Baldwin's book, *Henry Ford and the Jews: The Mass Production of Hate*, reveals. He believed that the "international Jew" was the source of the world's problems, and that "the international Jewish bankers arrange them [wars] so they can make money out of them." Ironically, this same theory has been advanced by conspiracy theorists against many secret societies, including the Freemasons.

 Famous Freemasons Past and Present

Benjamin Franklin
(1706–1790)

Initiated 1731, St. John's Lodge, Philadelphia

Scientist, inventor, statesman, printer, philosopher, and founding father, he joined the first recognized Masonic lodge in America in 1732, and was later made Provincial Grand Master of Pennsylvania. In 1734, he printed the first Freemasonic book to be published in America, an edition of Anderson's *Book of Constitutions*, the Bible for English Freemasonry. In the 1770s, he became Grand Master of the Nine Sisters Lodge in Paris, whose members included Danton, who played a vital role in the French Revolution, and the Marquis de Lafayette and Paul Jones, both of whom fought in the American War of Independence.

 Famous Freemasons Past and Present

Clark Gable (1901–1960)

Initiated 1933, Beverly Hills Lodge No. 528 California

The biggest box-office star of the early sound film era was a Shriner (the Ancient Arabic Order of the Nobles of the Mystic Shrine, an Order appendant to Freemasonry).

 Famous Freemasons Past and Present

CHAPTER 2
Inside the Lodge

A lodge is both the building where Masons meet and also a collective term for the Masons who meet there. Masons have met in lodges since the Middle Ages, when the great cathedrals were being built and the operative masons had special temporary buildings (called lodges—from the French word *loge* meaning "cabin") where they planned their work, received their pay, socialized during their leisure time, and slept.

Below: Freemasons' Annual General Meeting in 1992

EAST

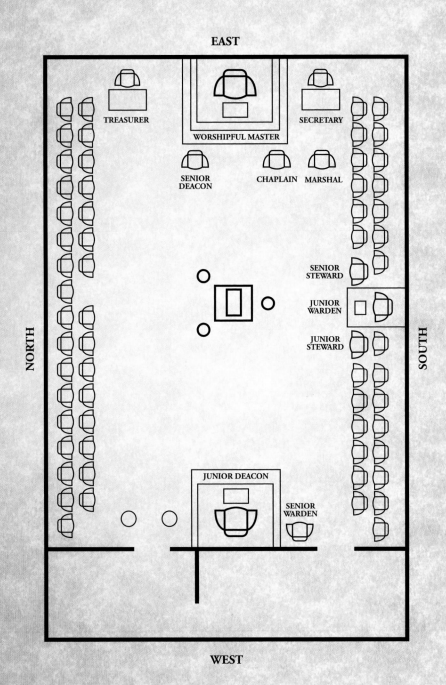

NORTH

SOUTH

WEST

Above: Diagram of a Masonic Lodge

Lodges are named for the town they are in, or for a famous Masonic figure. The name is always followed by a number, which is issued by the governing Grand Lodge in that area in order of when they received their charter. So the lodges with the smallest numbers are the oldest.

While there is some variation among them, lodges are always set up in the same geographical configuration, as shown in this diagram, in order to reproduce the scheme of the great Temple of Solomon (*see page 27*).

A Masonic lodge is rectangular with seating around the edges. The ceremonies take place in the center of the room. The lodge is oriented East to West, copying the orientation of ancient temples which were aligned with the rising and setting of the sun. Even if a Masonic lodge is not literally laid out in this way, symbolically when one enters the lodge one is facing East and Masonic meetings always start with the words, "In the East."

The three principal officers sit in specific places: the Worshipful Master in the East, the Senior Warden in the West, and the Junior Warden in the South. The Worshipful Master is in charge of the meetings and initiations, and sits on a triple throne on a dais of three steps, with the Marshal to his left and the Senior Deacon to his right. The Senior and Junior Deacons carry messages and assist in the rituals. The Senior and Junior Stewards also help to guide the new candidates in the initiation. The Tyler sits outside the door, armed with a sword, to prevent interruptions and to make sure that only Masons of the correct degree are allowed in.

In the center of the lodge, on a "mosaic pavement" consisting of black and white squares, sits the altar, covered with a crimson cloth that bears solar symbols. On the altar are a "volume of sacred law" (the Bible, Torah, or Koran, depending upon the majority faith of the lodge's membership), a Square, and Compasses. Three candles are positioned next to the altar to form a triangle.

There are two pillars on either side of the Senior Warden. These represent the two pillars at the entrance to the porch of King Solomon's Temple—"Boaz" (representing strength) on the left and "Jachin" (representing establishment) on the right.

Above the Worshipful Master's chair is suspended a letter "G" *(see page 36)*.

THE THIRTY-THREE DEGREES OF FREEMASONRY

Many people mistakenly believe that in order to become a Mason, one must be secretly approached by a practicing Mason and invited to join. Masons are actually forbidden from recruiting or even encouraging others to join the fraternity. Masons are allowed to talk to their friends about Masonry, why they enjoy it, and the good works that Freemasons perform, but they are instructed not to reveal any information about Masonic practices and rituals. The Masonic explanation for this is that becoming a Mason is a very personal choice, which affects how a person will live the rest of his life.

JOINING THE CRAFT

A person who wants to join should approach a Mason and ask for a petition. He fills this out and returns it to that Mason, who presents it to the lodge. The Master of the lodge then appoints a committee to undertake a background investigation and interview the applicant to find out more about him and his reasons for joining. Finally, the lodge votes on whether or not to accept him. The vote of acceptance must be unanimous. If a single lodge member rejects the applicant, the person is refused admission. If successful, the man is given a date on which he will perform the Entered Apprentice Degree. A Mason must profess belief in a Supreme Being; an atheist cannot become a Mason.

When the Entered Apprentice has completed all three degrees and paid the application fees for each one, he becomes a full member of the fraternity.

WHAT IS A DEGREE?

A degree is a stage or level of membership, the first three of which are Entered Apprentice, Fellow Craft, and Master Mason. Each degree teaches the brother a set of moral and spiritual lessons that he must assimilate in order to progress to the next degree.

Teaching takes place in the form of rituals, literature, and symbolism. Once a brother has completed the third degree he becomes a Master Mason and, purportedly, equal to all other Masons within the Craft. (For full descriptions of the three Blue Lodge rituals, *see pages 54-67.*)

As he progresses through the degrees, more signs, symbols, and "secrets" are revealed to him. A Master Mason supposedly knows everything there is to know, and the next thirty degrees of the Scottish Rite *(see page 31)* are merely refinements. This sounds very worthy in principle, but in practice a lot of senior Masons have admitted that there are secrets to which the rank-and-file have no access. In *The Brotherhood*, Stephen Knight reports that a highly-placed Mason told him, "Truth, to the initiate, is not for everyone; pearls must not be thrown before swine."

Much of the ritual of the first three degrees is dominated by fearful oaths of secrecy and the description of draconian sanctions. In fact, it could be argued that the whole of the Master Mason *(see page 193)* initiation ritual is designed to drive home this point, and actually casts the initiate in the role of the great architect (Hiram Abiff—*see page 15*) who died rather than reveal Masonic secrets. The rebirth which takes place at the end of the ritual, where the initiate is raised out of a coffin, sends a powerful message to the subconscious that death awaits the unfaithful, and that Masonic redemption is possible only through secrecy.

THE SCOTTISH AND YORK RITES

After completing the first three Symbolic degrees of Blue Lodge Masonry to become a Master Mason, a person may choose between two branches if he wishes to take further degrees.

One branch is called The Scottish Rite, which includes the fourth through the 32nd degrees. The Scottish Rite originated in France, not Scotland, and you don't have to be Scottish to follow it or to reach the 33rd degree.

The Scottish Rite degrees are lessons taught through elaborate plays in which the lodge is dressed up and lit, literally becoming the stage. The brethren have a specific dress code (costume) for each degree, and a specific set of tools and paraphernalia (props) are used. Candidates allegedly learn the lesson by watching the play.

The other branch of Freemasonry, known as the York Rite, consists of Royal Arch Masons, Royal and Select Masters, and Knights Templar (see page 95). The York Rite takes its name from the English city of York and is the link with the Saxon King, Athelstan, who converted to Christianity in York and is supposed to have granted the original charter to Masonic guilds in the city.

Ritual and role-playing are very powerful tools. Anti-Masons argue that the rituals are proof that Masonry is a dangerous cult that seeks to brainwash its members. Indeed, Masonry does meet some of the criteria associated with cults: the need for a special set of rules that you must obey or be cast out; calling each other "brother"; wearing unusual clothing; and using a specialized language. However, these are superficial criticisms that could just as easily be applied to other social clubs. Masonry does not try to distance initiates from their family and friends or demand that they give up personal goals. It does not seek to indoctrinate; rather, it encourages members to seek personal development. It has no charismatic living leader, and it does not recruit aggressively.

However, many critics argue that Masonry is pagan (*see page 72*), and there is still the nagging question of the Masonic hierarchy—there are a further thirty degrees that are numbered and named. Masons claim that this is not to imply that those who have achieved these degrees are of higher rank, but in practice it is difficult to see how this could be anything other than a hierarchical system of power and status, since each degree comes with its unique regalia including aprons, sashes, and hats. Hence the curious paradox of attainments: while it is advertised that the sublime degree of the Master Mason is the highest, it is an open secret that this is one of the lowest rungs on the Masonic ladder.

Right: George Washington Masonic National Monument

Johann Wolfgang von Goethe (1749–1832)

Initiated 1780, Lodge Amalia, Weimar, Germany

The giant of German literature—a man of genius who ranks with Shakespeare and Dante and the greatest thinkers of his age—became a Freemason when he was thirty years old. Six years earlier his international bestseller, *The Sorrows of Young Werther*, had made him a European sensation.

Maybe becoming a Mason was the natural progression for someone who, during his early twenties, had lived in Strasbourg, fallen in love with the cathedral, and immersed himself in the study of Gothic architecture.

There are many Masonic references in his work. One of his best-known Masonic poems is called "Masonic Lodge," which he wrote in his late sixties. He remained a practicing Freemason until his death in 1832. His last words were "more light!"

 Famous Freemasons Past and Present

Frederick the Great
(1712–1786)

Initiated 1738

He became a Freemason while he was still Crown Prince of Prussia, in 1738. In 1740, the first Masonic lodge in Prussia was formed.

In 1786, he issued "Grand Constitutions," which brought "The Ancient and Accepted Scottish Rite" into formal existence.

 Famous Freemasons Past and Present

Oliver Hardy (1892–1957)

Initiated Solomon Lodge No. 20, Jacksonville, Florida

Most famous for his association with Stan Laurel, he appeared in over 400 movies during his thirty-five-year career.

 Famous Freemasons Past and Present

Franz Haydn (1732–1809)

Initiated 1785, Lodge Zur Wahren Eintracht (True Harmony), Vienna, Austria

Initiated in his fifties, it was his friendship with Mozart, who was almost twenty-five years his junior and who had become a Mason two months earlier, which brought about his interest in Masonry. Mozart's father, Leopold, was also a member of this lodge. He wrote about his initiation in a letter dated February 2, 1785, to Count Aponyi: "Oh, how I wish it were Friday already. Oh, to feel the unspeakable joy of being among such worthy men!"

 Famous Freemasons Past and Present

J. Edgar Hoover (1895–1972)

Initiated 1920, Federal Lodge No. 1, Washington, D.C.

The infamous head of the Federal Bureau of Investigation (FBI) for nearly half a century, he became a Mason at the age of twenty-five and received numerous Masonic medals, awards, and decorations. He was a thirty-third degree Inspector General Honorary and was awarded the Scottish Rite's highest recognition, the Grand Cross of Honor, in 1965.

 Famous Freemasons Past and Present

CHAPTER 3
Secret Symbols

The public perception of Freemasonry is synonymous with its symbols: the apron, the rolled-up trouser legs, the compass and set square, the secret handshakes. At the first degree initiation ritual, the Entered Apprentice says, "Here, all is symbol." He acknowledges that he is beginning a journey during which more and more Masonic symbolism will be revealed to him as he progresses through the degrees.

In the Middle Ages, when illiteracy was widespread, symbolism was an important way of communicating ideas, a visual shorthand that could be understood by a cross-section of society, regardless of whether they could read or write. As literacy increased, the need for symbolism declined, so that by the twentieth century, although Masonic symbols were an integral part of the rites and rituals, their deeper meaning to the rank-and-file Masons had been lost. Critics argue that they had never been privy to the true meaning, and that this was revealed only to the elite at the 33rd degree and above. Apprentices are encouraged "to reach further" and "to gather what is scattered"; this appears over and over again in Masonic rites.

In *Symbols of Freemasonry,* Daniel Béresniak says, "The Rule, rites and symbols, allow every person to become themselves: to discover that they are all makers of meaning." Anti-Masons argue that the symbols are a way of hiding the truth and of protecting powerful and dangerous secret knowledge. This was necessary in the Masons' past when they were persecuted and needed to hide their knowledge.

He also says "Masonic symbolism is based on the notion of building, becoming, and making." "To make" is understood as "to make something of oneself."

However, Albert Pike, head of the Ancient Accepted Scottish Rite in the nineteenth century, said of the symbolism in *Morals and Dogma*: "The Blue Degrees are but the court or portico (porch) of the Temple. Part of the symbols are displayed there to the initiate, but he is intentionally misled by false interpretations. It is not intended that he shall understand them; but it is intended that he shall imagine that he understands them . . . their true explication (explanation and understanding) is reserved for the Adepts, the Princes of Masonry (those of the 32nd and 33rd degrees)."

This deception is also discussed by E.M. Storms, a Christian authority on Freemasonry, in his book *Should a Christian Be a Mason?* "Nowhere in Masonry is the 'brother' more cleverly deceived than in the presentation of its varied and ancient symbols. Most symbols are dualistic in nature and Masonic symbols are no exception. Behind all Masonic symbolism there is an undisclosed occult interpretation of which most Freemasons are ignorant."

Some critics take this apparent deception even further and believe that the symbolism is intended to blind the lower ranks to the real purpose of Lodge meetings. According to ex-32nd Degree Mason, William J. Schnoebelen, "Freemasonry is much like the fabled 'pyramid scheme.' It is a hierarchy in which the highest levels leech off the lower levels. Just as in the marketing schemes, the person at the top of the pyramid draws in most of the revenues because of the efforts of hundreds or thousands of people under him, so the same element works within the lodge . . . a Mason must spend hundreds of dollars, perhaps close to a thousand, to go through the degrees . . . there [is] a lot of free-floating cash somewhere up in the ranks."

There are over ninety symbols mentioned in the three lodge degrees. What is unclear is the powerful hidden meaning of these symbols, if any exists at all, beyond the accrued mysticism and mystery which has inevitably attached to them after centuries of use.

ALL-SEEING EYE

The ancient symbol of the mystical eye is not unique to Masonry. Although the all-seeing eye atop an unfinished pyramid appears on the original U.S. seal and the back of a U.S. one-dollar bill *(see page 143)*, the symbol was a familiar artistic convention for an "omniscient Ubiquitous Deity" in Renaissance art. For example, the frontispiece of Sir Walter Raleigh's *The History of the World* showed an eye in a cloud labeled "Providentia" overlooking a globe. From a Masonic perspective, the symbol is much more compli-cated than it at first appears. It has a cabalistic value of 70 plus 3 plus 200, equaling 273, which is the value of the phrase EHBEN MOSU HABONIM (the stone which the builders refused), familiar to all Royal Arch Masons. This value is also synonymous with Hiram Abiff, the architect of Solomon's Temple, who died before the temple was complete (hence the unfinished pyramid).

While it may represent the all-seeing deity, some anti-Masons argue that the Masonic interpretation places man in this omniscient position. Masonic writer J. D. Buck writes, in *Mystic Masonry* (1913), "It is far more important that men should strive to become Christs than they should believe that Jesus was Christ."

APRON

Made of pure white lambskin, the apron is the most important symbolic element in Masonry. It is worn by every Mason to all lodge events, and it is the first symbol to be explained to the Entered Apprentice. While it has developed from the larger protective apron worn by operative Masons in the Middle Ages, symbolically it is an emblem of innocence and the "badge of a Mason." It represents the purity of life, rectitude of conduct, and honor of constructive work and sacrifice.

Entered Apprentices wear the apron with the flap or bib raised up; Fellow Crafts wear the bib down. The Masters' aprons are made of hide or satin, lined with black and edged with red, green, or blue, depending on the rite.

In a Masonic funeral, the apron is placed on the mortal remains and buried with the body. In this respect, it is associated with the lamb of redemption and being born again, just as the Entered Apprentice is born again when he first accepts the apron.

CHECKERED / MOSAIC PAVEMENT

A checkered floor with alternating black and white squares, like a chessboard, takes an important place in the center of the floor of any Masonic lodge. Sometimes it covers the entire floor. It invites the Entered Apprentice to be mindful of the interplay of opposites: mercy and justice, reward and punishment, emotion and reason, revenge and love. Ultimately, it represents the deity as perceived in daily life.

Masonic texts of the eighteenth century refer to the Mosaic pavements as the "Moses" pavement, and other texts claim it is the pattern used on the part of the ground floor of Solomon's Temple where the high priest walked.

DOUBLE-HEADED EAGLE

The double-headed eagle has been used as a symbol of power for over 4,000 years and is part of the distinctive regalia of the 32nd and 33rd degrees of Scottish Rite Freemasonry. It is often called the "Eagle of Lagash," after its use in the ancient Sumerian city of Lagash. The symbol was assimilated by the Hittites, and then adopted by the Sleucid Turks and the Crusaders during the Middle Ages. The Emperor Charlemagne used the symbol in Europe, and it became an official Masonic symbol in 1758 by the body that called itself the Council of Emperors of the East and West.

But the double-headed eagle is more than merely a chivalric device, or a symbol of double jurisdiction. For Masons, it represents alchemical transformation, of the lowly and earthbound scorpion (the sign of Scorpio) into the soaring majestic creature. The eagle is also an alchemical symbol of purified sulfur and represents the ascending spirit. The two heads can be interpreted as the union between matter and spirit.

Gavel and Chisel

"Perhaps no lodge appliance or symbol is possessed of such deep and absorbing interest to the craft as the Master's mallet or gavel. Nothing in the entire range of Masonic paraphernalia and formulary can boast of an antiquity so unequivocally remote."

—*Joseph F. Ford*, Early History and Antiquities of Freemasonry

These tools are used to shape stone, or in symbolic terms, exert the will of the Mason over the materials, so the gavel and chisel are associated with conscience and the repeated effort and application of the active will. The gavel is a double-headed hammer that hits the chisel. The relationship between the active (gavel) and passive (chisel), which is directed by the force of the gavel, is evident. The gavel is used to keep order—in court, in auction houses, and in Masonic rituals—and it is a symbol of authority and power used by the Worshipful Master and his two Wardens. The gavel of the Master of a lodge is called a "Hiram," after the architect of Solomon's Temple, because it governs the Craft.

HEXAGRAM

This six-pointed star is made by combining the Earth Triangle and the Water Triangle. In Masonry, it is known as the Seal of Solomon. Masons claim that it represents harmony (much like the yin and yang symbol). It differs from the Star of David in that the triangles in the Masonic seal interlock.

Sexual connotations of the hexagram are explained by Albert G. Mackey in *The Symbolism of Freemasonry*. The Water Triangle is "a female symbol corresponding to the 'yoni' and the upward pointing triangle is the male, the 'lingam'. When the two triangles are interfaced, it represents the union of the active and passive forces in nature; it represents the male and female elements."

But more importantly, the hexagram is widely associated with the occult, and is considered the most powerful of Satan's symbols, containing "666." Occultists also call it the "trud" and use it in necromantic ceremonies to summon evil spirits.

PLUMB LINE AND PLUMB RULE

The plumb line is a piece of lead on a string and the plumb rule is the same item attached to a triangular frame. These tools are used to measure perpendiculars and horizontal axes. The triangle is a ubiquitous Masonic and occult symbol. A triangle that points downwards represents God (it is called the Deity's Triangle or Water Triangle). A triangle that points upwards is called the Earthly Triangle (also the Pyramid Triangle or Fire Triangle; it is the symbol of the Perfect or Divine Man, and famously appears in Mason Leonardo Da Vinci's *Vetruvian Man*). It is this triangle that is associated with the all-seeing eye *(see page 143)*. When the two triangles are combined, the resulting symbol is the hexagram.

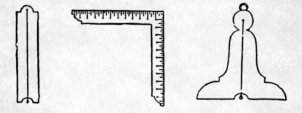

POINT WITHIN A CIRCLE

This is the important geometrical secret—the "secret of the square." Draw a circle and place a dot anywhere on the circumference. Then draw a line through the center of the circle that bisects the circumference. Finally, join the two places where the line meets the circumference with the dot to form a right angle. In the Middle Ages, the Master Mason would use this geometric principle to test the set squares of his workmen.

In speculative masonry, the symbol stands for the need to have true tools, education, standards, and morals.

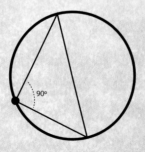

90°

ROUGH ASHLAR, PERFECT ASHLAR, AND POINTED CUBICAL STONE

Cutting stone is a symbolic act of "becoming." Rough ashlar is the Mason's raw material, unhewn stone to be worked with the Mason's tools. It symbolizes humans in their raw state, or rather the self that needs to be worked on through introspection and self-improvement. It can also be extended to highlight the importance of society and government:

"The rough Ashlar is the PEOPLE, as a mass, rude and unorganized. The perfect Ashlar, or cubical stone, symbol of perfection, is the STATE, the rulers deriving their powers from the consent of the governed; the constitution and laws speaking the will of the people; the government harmonious, symmetrical, efficient, its powers properly distributed and duly adjusted in equilibrium."
—*Albert Pike*, Morals and Dogma

Critics of Masonry draw attention to this symbol as a clear example of the way that Masonry expects its initiates to abandon individuality and turn themselves into identical building blocks (cubical stones) to create the edifice of Masonry. But Masons stress the opposite: that a brother should strive to construct a new self, think rationally, and find meaning on his own, in order to transform himself from the rough stone he had been before initiation, into a harmonious cubical stone (the Perfect Ashlar).

SEVEN SIX-POINTED STARS

The constellation of "Seven Six-pointed Stars" in Masonry represents the seven liberal arts and sciences: grammar, rhetoric, logic, arithmetic, geometry, music, and astronomy.

SQUARE AND THE COMPASS

These are the most widely recognized symbols of Masonry, and on one level they represent the relationship between mind and matter, and on another the relationship between emotions and reason. They are ancient symbols of metaphysical creation. Art from as early as the Middle Ages depicts God as the divine architect, creating the universe with these tools.

"He took the golden compasses, prepared
In God's eternal store, to circumscribe
The Universe, and all created things . . ."
—*John Milton,* Paradise Lost

Blue Lodge Masons are taught that they should be "square" in their dealings with others and that they should "circumscribe their passions." But, as with many dualistic symbols, these symbols can also be interpreted in sexual and pagan terms. The square represents the female earth principle, and the compass the more spiritual and mindful male. The phallic compass is positioned above the receptive square to indicate male dominance over and impregnation of the female.

Although there are female Masonic lodges, it appears that the key Masonic symbol is a constant reminder of the dominance of men over women.

TWENTY-FOUR-INCH GAUGE

This is a ruler two-feet long, divided into twenty-four parts, each one inch in length. The operative Masons used it to measure their stone, but symbolically it is a persistent reminder of mortality and the need to use time wisely and constructively.

"The twenty-four inch gauge is an instrument made use of by operative Masons, to measure and lay out their work; but Free and Accepted Masons are taught to make use of it for the more noble and glorious purpose of dividing their time; it being divided into twenty-four equal parts, is emblematical of the twenty-four hours of the day, which they are taught to divide into three equal parts; whereby are found eight hours for the service of God and a distressed worthy brother; eight hours for their usual avocations; and eight for refreshment and sleep."
—*Thomas Smith Webb*, Freemason's Monitor *(1797)*

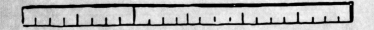

"Les Free-Masons" by Bernard Picart from Histoire des Religions

Harry Houdini
(1874–1926)

Initiated 1923, St. Cecile Lodge No. 568, New York

Born Ehrich Weiss, the son of Hungarian immigrants, this master showman, with a genius for publicity, spent more than two decades in the limelight as an escape artist and is remembered today as the world's most famous magician. In later years, he spent much of his time debunking spiritualism and exposing psychic frauds.

 Famous Freemasons Past and Present

Edward Jenner
(1749–1823)

Initiated 1802, Royal Faith and Friendship Lodge No. 270, Berkeley, Gloucestershire, England

This English surgeon and Fellow of the Royal Society is known for discovering the scientific principles of vaccination and a vaccine for smallpox. He served as Worshipful Master for the Royal Faith and Friendship Lodge. In 1825, six lodges raised funds to erect a statue of him inside the west door of Gloucester Cathedral.

 Famous Freemasons Past and Present

Al Jolson (1886–1950)

Initiated St. Cecile Lodge No. 568, New York

Born Asa Yoelson in Lithuania, his parents immigrated to the United States at the end of the nineteenth century. The master showman of American theater and movies was a Mason and a staunch patriot, who was posthumously awarded the Congressional Medal of Merit for his contribution towards bolstering the morale of frontline troops during the two world wars.

 Famous Freemasons Past and Present

Charles Lindbergh (1902–1974)

Initiated Keystone Lodge No. 243, St. Louis, Missouri

Lindbergh was the heroic American aviator who, in 1927, became the first person to complete a solo nonstop flight across the Atlantic. His image has been tarnished by his admiration of Hitler's policies (he received the Service Cross of the German Eagle in 1938). In 1939, he wrote a *Readers' Digest* article entitled "Aviation, Geography and Race" in which he said, "We can have peace and security only as long as we band together to preserve . . . our inheritance of European blood, only so long as we guard ourselves against attack by foreign armies and dilution by foreign races."

 Famous Freemasons Past and Present

CHAPTER 4

The Masonic Handshake

During the Middle Ages, a series of handshakes were introduced to enable Masons to identify each other, and to prevent fraudsters from passing themselves off as skilled craftsmen. Today, the Masonic handshake, or "grip," is taught to Blue Lodge Masons during the three initiation ceremonies.

For the first three degrees of Freemasonry there is not one grip, but five. There are also other poses known as the "dueguard" and "sign" that differ for each degree, and are used to salute the Worshipful Master and gain entry to the lodge. In this chapter all of these secret signs will be revealed.

During the initiation ceremony for each degree, a candidate is shown the grip, due-guard, and sign that correspond to that degree. No one is allowed to be present, in any degree of Masonry, unless they are of that same degree or higher. So these grips are used to demonstrate that a Brother has reached a certain degree and can be privy to the business of that meeting.

The lodge looks the same when it is open on the first, second, or third degree, so it is the Tyler's duty to inform all brethren of what degree the lodge is open. This is especially important when members have arrived late, so that they do not give the wrong sign to the Worshipful Master. For example, if the lodge were open on the first degree, a Master Mason must be informed of this by the Tyler; otherwise, he might inadvertently give the sign for the third degree, and reveal it accidentally to those Entered Apprentices who are present.

Anyone arriving late will approach the Tyler, who stands guard outside the room, sword in hand. They ask the Tyler on what degree the lodge is open, put on their apron, and ask the Tyler to admit them. The Tyler knocks once if the lodge is open at the first degree, twice if the lodge is open at the second degree, and three times if the lodge is open at the third degree. The Junior Deacon opens the door and announces, "Worshipful Master, there is an alarm at the inner door of our lodge." The Worshipful Master replies, "Attend to the alarm, Brother Junior, and ascertain the cause." The Tyler reports the names of the brothers to the Junior Deacon and they are admitted. They must then walk to the center of the lodge and perform the appropriate dueguard and sign at the altar, to which the Worshipful Master responds with the same.

No brother can sit down until he has saluted the Worshipful Master in this way with the corresponding dueguard and sign.

ENTERED APPRENTICE DEGREE

DUEGUARD OF AN ENTERED APPRENTICE ⊢······▶

The dueguard of an Entered Apprentice represents the position of the hands when taking the oath of an Entered Apprentice, "my left hand supporting the Bible and my right hand resting thereon."

⊢ *SIGN OF AN ENTERED APPRENTICE*

The sign of the Entered Apprentice refers to the penalty the Entered Apprentice will suffer if he divulges Masonic secrets:

". . . binding myself under no less a penalty than that of having my throat cut across, my tongue torn out, and with my body buried in the sands of the sea at low-water mark, where the tide ebbs and flows twice in twenty-four hours, should I ever knowingly or willfully violate this, my solemn Obligation of an Entered Apprentice."

1. Raise your right arm to neck-level with a flat palm facing downward.
2. Draw your arm sharply across your neck.
3. Drop your arm to your side.

GRIP (HANDSHAKE) OF AN ENTERED APPRENTICE: "BOAZ"

The grip of the Entered Apprentice is made by pressing the thumb against the top of the first knuckle-joint of the other Mason; the other Mason reciprocates.

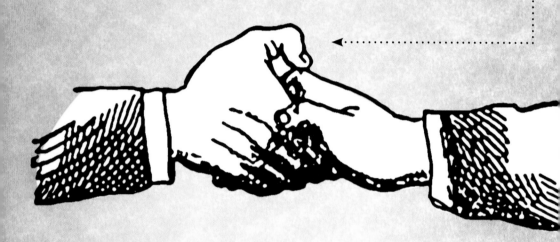

The name of this grip is "Boaz," which is described as "a certain friendly or brotherly grip, whereby one Mason may know another in the dark as in the light."

Boaz (representing strength) is the name of the pillar on the left of the entrance to the porch of King Solomon's Temple.

FELLOW CRAFT DEGREE

DUEGUARD OF THE FELLOW CRAFT

The dueguard of a Fellow Craft represents the position of the hands when taking the oath of the Fellow Craft degree, "my right hand on the Holy Bible, square, and compasses, my left arm forming an angle, supported by the square and my hand in a vertical position."

1. Raise your left hand above your head and to the side so that it forms a right angle, with flat palm facing forward.
2. The right arm forms a square in front of and not touching the body, with the open palm facing downward.

SIGN OF A FELLOW CRAFT

The sign of the Fellow Craft refers to the penalty the Fellow Craft will suffer if he divulges Masonic secrets:

". . . binding myself under no less a penalty than that of having my left breast torn open, my heart and vitals taken thence, and with my body given as a prey to the vultures of the air, should I ever knowingly or willfully violate this, my solemn Obligation of a Fellow Craft."

1. Raise your left hand above your head and to the side so that it forms a right angle, with flat palm facing forward.
2. Cup your right hand over your left breast.
3. Draw your right hand quickly across your body.
4. Drop your right hand sharply to the side.
5. Drop your left hand sharply to the side.

PASS GRIP (HANDSHAKE) OF A FELLOW CRAFT: "SHIBBOLETH"

The pass grip of the Fellow Craft is made by pressing the thumb against the space between the first and second knuckle joints of the first two fingers of the other Fellow Craft; the other Fellow Craft reciprocates.

The name of this grip is "shibboleth." The origin of the use of the word "shibboleth" as a password and means of identifying one group from another is recorded in chapter twelve of the biblical Book of Judges. In ancient Hebrew dialects, the word "shibboleth" meant "ear of grain." In some dialects it was pronounced with a *sh* sound, and in others it was pronounced with an *s*.

After a battle between two Semitic tribes, the Ephraimites and the Gileadites, the latter set up a blockade to catch the fleeing and vanquished Ephraimites. The sentry guards challenged each person they stopped to pronounce the word "shibboleth." Those who pronounced it with an *s* could be identified as Ephraimites, since the Gileadites used the *sh* pronunciation.

"Then Jephthah gathered together all the men of Gilead, and fought with Ephraim . . . And the Gileadites took the passages of Jordan before the Ephraimites: and it was so, that when those Ephraimites which were escaped said, Let me go over; that the men of Gilead said unto him, Art thou an Ephraimite? If he said, Nay; Then said they unto him, Say now Shibboleth: and he said Sibboleth: for he could not frame to pronounce it right. Then they took him, and slew him at the passages of Jordan: and there fell at that time of the Ephraimites forty and two thousand."

—Judges 12:4

REAL GRIP (HANDSHAKE) OF A FELLOW CRAFT: "JACHIN"

The real grip of the Fellow Craft is made by pressing the thumb against the second knuckle of the other Fellow Craft; the other Fellow Craft reciprocates.

The name of this grip is "Jachin." Jachin (representing establishment) is the name of the pillar on the right of the entrance to the porch of King Solomon's Temple. In I Kings 7:15,16 we are told that the two pillars (Jachin and Boaz) measured eighteen cubits plus five cubits for the capitals, a total height of twenty-three cubits for each pillar.

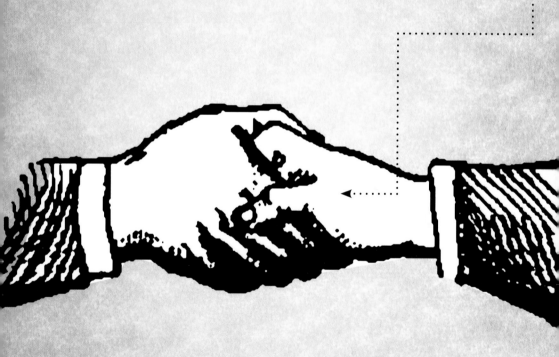

MASTER MASON DEGREE

DUEGUARD OF A MASTER MASON

The dueguard of a Master Mason represents the position of the hands when taking the oath of the Master Mason Degree, "both hands resting on the Holy Bible, square, and compasses."

1. Raise both arms in front of you, open palms facing downward, so that your upper arms and forearms form a right angle.

SIGN OF A MASTER MASON

The sign of the Master Mason refers to the penalty the Master Mason will suffer if he divulges Masonic secrets:

". . . binding myself under no less a penalty than that of having my body severed in two, my bowels taken from thence and burned to ashes, and the ashes thereof scattered to the four winds of heaven, that there might remain neither track, trace nor remembrance among man or Masons of so vile and perjured a wretch as I should be should I ever knowingly or willfully violate this, my solemn Obligation of a Master Mason."

1. The right arm forms a square in front of and not touching the body, with the open palm facing downward.
2. Draw the thumb quickly across the waist to the right hip.
3. Drop the hand to your side.

PASS GRIP (HANDSHAKE) OF A MASTER MASON: "TUBALCAIN"

The pass grip of the Master Mason is made by pressing the thumb against the space between the second and third knuckle joints of the other Fellow Craft; the other Fellow Craft reciprocates.

The name of this grip is "Tubalcain." In the Bible (Genesis 4:22), Tubalcain is described as the son of Lamech and Zillah, "an instructor of every artificer [cutting instrument] in brass and iron." As a skilled metalworker, his name has relevance to the construction of the metal pillars of Boaz and Joachin, and also the many other metal furnishings and objects that were inside the temple.

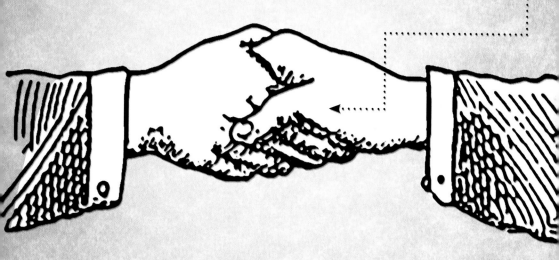

REAL GRIP (HANDSHAKE) OF A MASTER MASON: "MA-HA-BONE"

This grip is also known as the "Strong Grip of the Master Mason" or the "Lion's Paw." Just after he has been "raised," a Master Mason is instructed for this grip at the "graveside" as follows:

1. Firmly grasp the right hand of the other Master Mason.
2. Interlace the thumbs of both hands.
3. Place the top two fingers against the fleshy part of the thumb.
4. Place the bottom two fingertips against the wrist of the other Master Mason where it meets the hand.
5. Press the tips of your fingers firmly against the other Master Mason's hand.

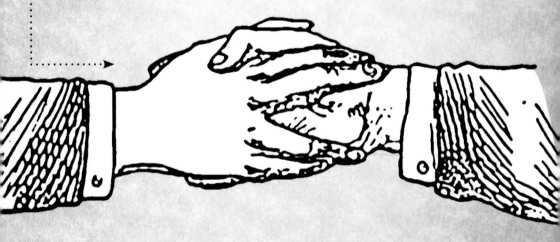

THE FIVE POINTS OF FELLOWSHIP

During initiation into the Master Mason degree, after the candidate has received the pass grip of a Master Mason, he is "raised," or resurrected, at the end of the enactment of the Hiramic Legend.

The Worshipful Master grasps the hand of the candidate and, by using the real grip of the Master Mason, "raises" him from the dead to the position known as the Five Points of Fellowship.

The Worshipful Master and candidate embrace one another while adopting five positions: foot to foot; knee to knee; breast to breast; hand to back; and cheek to cheek, or mouth to ear.

The Worshipful Master whispers the words "Ma-Ha-Bone" into the candidate's ear (derived from "Macbenae," which means "the flesh falls from the bone." Another interpretation is "What! The Builder."). This is the substitute secret word. The candidate has experienced resurrection. He is then shown the real grip or Lion's Paw of a Master Mason and utters the following oath:

"I do promise and swear that I will not give the substitute for the Master's Word in any other way or manner than that in which I receive it, which will be on the Five Points of Fellowship, and at low breath."

GRAND HAILING SIGN OF DISTRESS ⌐ ·

After receiving instruction in the grips, signs, and the Five Points of Fellowship of the
Master Mason, the candidate is taught the Grand Hailing Sign of Distress.

1. Raise both hands toward heaven, with each arm
   forming the angle of a square, or a ninety-degree angle,
   with flat palms facing forward.
2. Lower the arms in three distinct motions to the sides, so
   the arms come to rest naturally on either side of the body.

If a Master Mason in distress is in a place where the Grand Hailing Sign of Distress
cannot be seen, he may utter a verbal substitute for the sign:

"O Lord, my God, is there no help for the Widow's Son?"

The sign and the words should never be used together. The candidate also utters
the oath:

*"Furthermore, I do promise and swear that I will not give the Grand
Hailing Sign of Distress of a Master Mason, except for the benefit of
the Craft while at work or for the instruction of a Brother, unless I
am in real distress; and if ever I should see it given, or hear the words
accompanying it, by a worthy brother in distress, I will fly to his relief,
if there is a greater probability of saving his life than losing my own."*

A Freemason initiation ritual

Wolfgang Amadeus Mozart (1756–1791)

Initiated 1784, Lodge Zur Woltatigkeit,
Vienna, Austria

During the period of Mozart's lifetime, Masonry was prominent in Viennese society. Mozart himself was eleven years of age when he composed a song set to a Masonic poem, "An die Freude," for Dr. Joseph Wolf, a Mason who had treated him for smallpox.

Mozart's father was a Mason, and Mozart wrote "Fellow Crafts Journey" (Op. K468) in honor of his father receiving his second degree of Masonry on April 16, 1785. During his lifetime he wrote several other pieces for Masonry, but the opera "The Magic Flute" is his most famous piece with Masonic references.

It is well known for its Masonic content, but the references are mainly concerned with the first degree of entered apprentice. Some parts of the opera seem overly elaborate and impenetrable, without an understanding of Masonic symbolism. Emanuel Schikaneder, the librettist who also played Papageno in the first performances, was also a Mason. Obvious Masonic elements include the ritual initiation at the beginning of Act Two and the subsequent ceremonies and trial.

The first performance of the "The Magic Flute" took place on September 30, 1791. Some scholars believe that Mozart knew that Masonry would soon be outlawed in Vienna, so he used the "The Magic Flute" as a way of encoding the esoteric knowledge that he had learnt as a Mason.

 Famous Freemasons Past and Present

Horatio Nelson
(1758–1805)
Initiated York Lodge No. 256

The son of the village rector, he won fame as a leading naval commander for his bold and unorthodox tactics, but it was his death at the Battle of Trafalgar that made him one of Britain's greatest national heroes.

In 1839, the *Freemasons' Quarterly Review* claimed Nelson was a Freemason, and Hamon Le Strange, in his *History of Freemasonry in Norfolk*, says there is a stone with an inscription to Nelson among the furniture of the Lodge of Friendship No. 100 at Yarmouth which reads: "In Memory of Bro. V. Nelson of the Nile, and of Burnham Thorpe, in Norfolk, who lost his life in the army of Victory, in an engagement with ye Combin'd Fleets of France and Spain, off Cape Trafalgar, Oct. 21, 1805. Proposed by Bro. John Cutlove."

 Famous Freemasons Past and Present

CHAPTER 5
Pagan Rites

The questions most frequently asked about Freemasonry are: Is it a separate religion? Is it compatible with other faiths? Is it essentially pagan, or even Satanic, in nature?

The *American Heritage® Dictionary of the English Language* defines a religion as an "... institutionalized system grounded in the belief in and reverence for a supernatural power or powers regarded as creator and governor of the universe."

Freemasonry seems to fit this broad definition easily, but what we are really asking when we pose this question is, "Is Freemasonry a separate religion?" Freemasons always argue that Masonry is not a religion, and they often bring other conditions into the debate to define religion. Many Masons argue that to be a religion an organization must propose its unique plan for salvation or path by which one reaches the after-life; it must have a theology which attempts to describe the nature of God and the way in which we should communicate with God.

"The term 'mystery religion' means that it is a religion in which elements are kept hidden from the 'profane' (non-members). You can only learn these elements by going through a formal initiation in which you are ceremonially set apart from the masses and sworn formally to secrecy. Only then are you entrusted with the group's secrets, and then in degrees."
—William J. Schnoebelen

John J. Robinson, author of *Born in Blood: The Lost Secrets of Freemasonry*, expresses this conventional Masonic idea: "In the ceremonies and lectures that lead to a man being raised to the status of Master Mason, he hears no description of heaven or hell. He hears no religious dogma. He hears no mention of Satan. He is told of no Masonic pathway to salvation for the simple reason that there is none. The only religious item in the Masonic lodge is the holy book of the initiate's own faith."

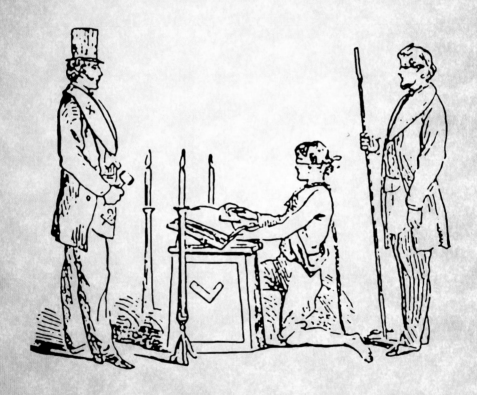

Above: A blindfolded initiate is sworn in

"The Masonic Movement . . . is a far more occult organization than can be realized, and is intended to be the training school for the coming advanced occultists. In its ceremonials lies hid the wielding of the forces connected with the growth and life of the kingdoms of nature and the unfoldment of the divine aspects of man."

—*Alice Ann Bailey,* The Externalization of the Hierarchy

Anti-Masons often cite prominent Mason Albert G. Mackey's entry in the *Encyclopedia of Freemasonry* as proof that Freemasonry is indeed a religion: "I contend, without any sort of hesitation, that Masonry is, in every sense of the word [a religion], except one, and that its least philosophical, an eminently religious institution—that it is indebted solely to the religious element which it contains for its origin and for its continued existence, and that without this religious element it would scarcely be worthy of cultivation by the wise and good."

They also claim (like Stephen Knight) that Freemasonry deceives men of other faiths into believing that they are worshipping their own God, when in fact the Masonic God is a triune deity called "Jahbulon": *Jah*, for the Hebrew god Yahweh; *Bul*, for the ancient Canaanite fertility god Baal and devil; and *On*, for Osiris, the Egyptian god of the underworld.

Is Freemasonry Compatible with Other Faiths?

Carl J. Sanders, Bishop of the United Methodist Church and holder of the highest honor conferred by the Scottish Rite of Freemasonry, sees no conflict between his religion and his membership in Freemasonry: "My Masonic activities have never interfered with my loyalty to and my love for my Church. Quite to the contrary, my loyalty to my Church has been strengthened by my Masonic ties. Good Masons are good Churchmen."

However, the Catholic Church has forbidden its members from becoming Freemasons. On April 28, 1738, Pope Clement XII, in his Pontifical Constitution "In Eminenti," condemned Freemasonry as being Counter-Church and Counter-State.

This extreme position has not changed and many subsequent Popes have restated it. In 1917, Canon 2335 of the *Code of Canon Law* stated, "Those who join a Masonic sect or other societies of the same sort, which plot against the Church or against legitimate civil authority, incur *ipso facto* an excommunication simply reserved to the Holy See."

Some Church statements have watered down this admonition by saying that Catholics should not join societies which seek to destroy or plot against the church. But as recently as 1983 the Church reiterated, "[Masonic] principles have always been considered irreconcilable with the doctrine of the Church and, therefore, membership in them remains forbidden. The faithful, who enroll in Masonic associations are in a state of grave sin and may not receive Holy Communion." Pope Benedict XVI expressed his opposition to Freemasonry several times when he was a Cardinal.

In 2002, the Archbishop of Canterbury, Dr. Rowan Williams, said he believed Christianity and Freemasonry to be "incompatible" and admitted, "I have real misgivings about the compatibility of Masonry and Christian profession . . . I have resisted the appointment of known Masons to certain senior posts."

"There are highly occult elements woven into the very warp and woof of Freemasonry. Thus, the Lodge is not just 'another religion' like the Muslims or the Buddhists—although that alone should be enough to keep Christians from involving themselves in it. The nature and character of the Lodge's deepest theological underpinnings are rooted in Witchcraft and Paganism."
—William J. Schnoebelen

The Muslim faith is equally critical of Freemasonry, owing in part to suspicions that the ultimate goal of the Freemasons is to rebuild the Temple of Solomon on its original site in Jerusalem, a place currently occupied by the Al-Aqsa Mosque.

Muslim scholar Sheikh Ahmad Kutty, a Senior Lecturer and Islamic Scholar at the Islamic Institute of Toronto in Ontario, Canada, gives reasons why Muslims should not be Freemasons: "Freemasonry is a secret organization whose beliefs and practices are totally kept confidential except from those who are initiated into it. They have levels of secrets which are not divulged to those who are at lower levels. A Muslim should never fall prey or give allegiance to something which cannot be scrutinized by the firm criteria of the Qur'an and the Sunnah. Whoever joins Freemasonry is like a person who writes a blank check; by doing so he agrees to give allegiance blindly to an authority to comply with their wishes no matter what they are."

IS FREEMASONRY PAGAN AND/OR SATANIC?

The word "pagan" has been loaded with negative associations ever since the Christian Church launched its campaign to vilify and destroy non-Christian religions during its ascendancy. The word "pagan" has come to mean anyone who follows a religion which is not Christian, Muslim, or Jewish, and is applied especially to polytheistic religions. The label "pagan" also includes a hedonistic pejorative element. Freemasonry definitely contains pagan elements—not least the importance of Hiram Abiff and Egyptian and Gnostic influences. So perhaps the question needs to be refined as "Do Masons worship a pagan or Satanic god?"

"The occult revival of the twentieth century can be directly attributed to Freemasonry and its peripheral entourage of acolytes: Theosophy, the New Age Movement, Satanism, Cabalistic Black Magic, Enochian Magic, Gerardian Wicca, Alexandrian Wicca and Sex Magic."
—Terry Melanson

In *The Lost Keys of Freemasonry*, 33rd degree Mason Manly P. Hall says, "The true Mason is not creed-bound. He realizes with the divine illumination of his lodge that as a Mason his religion must be universal: Christ, Buddha or Mohammed, the name means little, for he recognizes only the light and not the bearer . . . The Masonic order is not a mere social organization, but is composed of all those who have banded themselves together to learn and apply the principles of mysticism and the occult rites."

This emphasis on "the light and not the bearer" has been seized on by anti-Masons to claim that Freemasonry worships the sun.

As we have seen in other parts of this book, the sun does feature heavily in Masonic ritual and the nineteenth-century Masonic preoccupation with obelisks (see page 162) and the orientation of the Lodge (see page 27) would seem to bear this out.

"All truly dogmatic religions have issued from the Kabalah and return to it: everything scientific and grand in the religious dreams of all the Illuminati . . . is borrowed from the Kabalah; all the Masonic associations owe to it their Secrets and their Symbols."
—Albert Pike

Above: Satan in one of his many forms

The source of many anti-Masonic accusations of paganism have been in response to the writing of Manly P. Hall, Albert Pike, and Dr. Albert Mackey, all of whom could be described as self-taught mystics who wrote reams of material about Freemasonry and the ancient mysteries. Pike is considered to be a guru by many Freemasons, while a large number of non-Masons view him as a Luciferian, preaching a secret doctrine hidden from the majority of Blue Lodge Masons. Many pro-Masonic sources have tried to lessen the impact of these writings by claiming that they discussed paganism and occultism without a proper understanding of the Craft, and claim that Mackey, in later years, made a retraction of his former paganistic doctrines. While it is true to say that both men were writing at a time when interest in the occult was commonplace, they should not be dismissed completely. A society should be defined in terms of its members, and while many would undoubtedly find paganism abhorrent, it isn't beyond the bounds of probability that Masonry still attracts a sizeable number of occultists.

Many anti-Masonic books have printed a letter which has been attributed to Albert Pike in which says that all Masons are secret followers of Lucifer:

Above: Part of a Masonic initiation ritual

"That which we must say to a crowd is—We worship a God, but it is the God that one adores without superstition.

To you, Sovereign Grand Inspectors General, we say this, that you may repeat it to the Brethren of the 32nd, 31st, and 30th degrees—The Masonic Religion should be, by all of us initiates of the high degrees, maintained in the purity of the Luciferian Doctrine.

If Lucifer were not God, would Adonay whose deeds prove his cruelty, perfidy and hatred of man, barbarism and repulsion for science, would Adonay and his priests, calumniate him?

Yes, Lucifer is God, and unfortunately Adonay is also God. For the eternal law is that there is no light without shade, no beauty without ugliness, no white without black, for the absolute can only exist as two gods: darkness being necessary to the statue, and the brake to the locomotive.

Thus, the doctrine of Satanism is a heresy; and the true and pure philosophical religion is the belief in Lucifer, the equal of Adonay; but Lucifer, God of Light and God of Good, is struggling for humanity against Adonay, the God of Darkness and Evil."

However, this letter is actually thought to have been written by Gabriel Jogand-Pages, and he admitted it was a hoax in 1897. The debate about Freemasonry's pagan roots and religious practices will continue for many years to come.

Freemasons at the Paris Commune, a working-class uprising that threatened the French government in 1871

Alexander Pushkin
(1799–1837)
Initiated 1821, Lodge Ovid, Kischinev, Russia

Masonry came to Russia in the second half of the eighteenth century and was widespread among intellectuals. The coup in December 1825 against the new tsar by the "Decembrists" was orchestrated by the Masons. According to Michael Howard, in *The Occult Conspiracy*, the "Decembrists" were officers and intellectuals whose lodges had been outlawed by Tsar Alexander I three years previously. Count Pushkin was one of these revolutionary Masons.

 Famous Freemasons Past and Present

Franklin Delano Roosevelt (1882–1945)

Initiated 1911, Holland Lodge No. 8, New York

F.D.R., the thirty-second president of the United States, was a member of the same lodge where George Washington held honorary membership.

Some of the more extreme conspiracy theorists claim that not only were Churchill and F.D.R. Masons, but so was Stalin, and that when these three world leaders got together at Yalta in February 1945, Stalin ended up with a huge chunk of Eastern Europe because they were laying the Masonic foundation stone for the third world war, which will allegedly take place between Judaism and Islam, resulting in the New World Order as foreseen by the nineteenth-century Masonic giant, Albert Pike *(see page 154)*.

 Famous Freemasons Past and Present

Sir Walter Scott (1771–1832)

Initiated 1801, Saint David Lodge No. 36, Edinburgh, Scotland

Scott was the Scottish novelist and poet and author of *Ivanhoe*, one of the most important literary works of all time. This novel describes the ancient tensions between Jews, Christians, and Muslims and forms the basis of many people's knowledge of the mysterious Knights Templar.

 Famous Freemasons Past and Present

CHAPTER 6
Covert Cousins

The Freemasons are the largest fraternal organization in existence. Membership reached a peak in the 1950s, but even today there are nearly six million Masons worldwide, with half of this number based in the United States.

However, controversy has always followed Freemasonry, and it is sometimes aggravated by the stubborn refusal of the Masons to address accusations of unsavory practices head-on. Sometimes, it chooses to maintain a dignified silence and avoids engaging in dialogue with the opponents of Freemasonry; other times it goes to such great lengths to improve its image (it recently hired a Public Relations company) that it draws further accusations of attempting a cover-up or being too vocal in defense of its practices. Masonic materials produced for public consumption are often suspected of being propaganda tools and just another part of a deceptive Masonic public relations program.

The history of Freemasonry, its affiliations, and secret societies within societies, is intimately tied with all the other major esoteric or chivalric groups of the last two thousand years. Its hierarchical structure has been copied and adapted by many other orders, and as Jim Marrs says in *Rule by Secrecy*, "The ongoing connective tissue between the modern and ancient secret societies has been Freemasonry."

Right: An initiate is led blindfolded into a Freemason lodge

The reason the Freemasons were so important during the Middle Ages was because, at a time when any movements which opposed the Holy Roman Universal (Catholic) Church were forced underground, the guilds of stone masons were able to move freely around Europe. They had lodges in every major city and therefore their ideas could be spread with relative ease: "Already possessing certain esoteric or secret knowledge, the Masons were an ideal vehicle for the covert distribution of anticlerical teachings."

THE ILLUMINATI

Some people believe this is the most powerful of all secret societies, and that today it still survives hidden deep within Freemasonry, seeking to form a federal Europe and then a single world government. Others go even further and allege that it is the personal coven of the Rothschilds, the richest family on the planet.

The Illuminati was founded in the eighteenth century by Dr. Adam Weishaupt, who was born the son of a Jewish rabbi in 1748. He later converted to Catholicism, trained to become a priest, and then became an atheist who harbored a life-long fascination with the Jesuit theology that had been instrumental in his upbringing. He founded the secret Order of the Illuminati in 1776, with headquarters in Munich, allegedly under the direction of the recently formed House of Rothschild, as a coalition of liberalism and the furthering of knowledge.

"Illuminati" means "enlightened ones," and there are many explanations for its origins. It could be derived from Luciferian teachings (Lucifer means "Bearer of Light"), since Weishaupt was well versed in anti-Christian doctrines, astrology, and the occult; alternatively, Weishaupt may have taken the name from a secret Spanish Jesuit splinter group called the "Alumbrados" ("enlightened"), founded by Ignatius Loyola. This group taught a form of Gnosticism which believed that formal religion was unnecessary for those who intuitively apprehended spiritual truths. These were dangerous beliefs which had attracted persecution from the Spanish Inquistion in the seventeenth century and were no less heretical for Weishaupt.

Left: The All-seeing eye, the alleged symbol of the Illuminati

The Masonic symbol "G" may well stand for "God" but, with the influence of the Illuminati, it must also be synonymous with "Gnosticism." The Illuminati began with just five members. It copied the hierarchical structure of the Freemasons, but a year later, in 1777, it burrowed its way into Freemasonry and some believe it continues to this day as a secret society within a secret society pulling the strings. This is confirmed by one of Weishaupt's letters to a fellow Illuminati written in 1794: "The great strength of our Order lies in its concealment. Let it never appear in any place in its own name, but always covered by another name, and another occupation. None is fitter than the three lower degrees of Freemasonry; the public is accustomed to it, expect little from it, and therefore take little notice of it."

In 1777, Weishaupt and his illuminated associates joined the Masonic Lodge Theodore of Good Counsel in Munich, as the French Revolutionary leader and Illuminati member Mirabeau (Honoré-Gabriel Riqueti, Comte de Mirabeau) reveals in his memoirs: "[they] resolved to graft on to their branch another secret association to which they gave the name of the Order of the Illumines." Six years later, the Illuminati philosophy infiltrated Masonic lodges throughout Europe and even America, after the Bavarian government cracked down on the order, causing many members to flee Germany.

Even the Masonic Founding Father, Thomas Jefferson, was taken in by Weishaupt, whom he described in glowing terms: "[he] seems to be an enthusiastic philanthropist. Weishaupt believes that to promote the perfection of the human character was the object of Jesus Christ."

Weishaupt's ultimate goal was, of course, power, and he achieved this very effectively through a secret and powerful pyramid chain of command. In documents seized by the Bavarian authorities he described his power structure: "I have two immediately below me into whom I breathe my whole spirit, and each of these two has again two others, and so on. In this way I can set a thousand men in motion and on fire in the simplest manner, and in this way one must impart orders and operate on politics."

By 1790, the Illuminati appeared to have fallen apart. In reality, its members were spread all over the world. As American journalist William T. Still points out, "Even though the Illuminati faded from public view, the monolithic apparatus set in motion by Weishaupt may still exist today. Certainly, the goals and methods of operation still exist. Whether the name Illuminati still exists is really irrelevant."

Many researchers believe that because the Illuminati infected its Masonic hosts so effectively, its New World agenda—which includes the abolition of all government, private property, nationalism, organized religion, and the family unit—is still very much alive today.

ROSICRUCIANS

This movement developed in the early sixteenth century when several like-minded free-thinkers, alchemists, Christian Kabbalists, and rational humanists came together to form a blend of mystical Christianity and enlightenment scholarship. One of the forerunners of the group is believed to be the renowned Moravian alchemist Michael Sendivogius, whose Society of the Unknown Philosophers published *Twelve Treatises on the Philosophers' Stone* in 1604. However, it would be another century before they came to public notice and became known as the Rosicrucians (followers of the Rosy-cross). Some people believe that they never existed and are the fictitious creation of an allegorical pamphlet. However, it is more likely that the individuals dissolved into Freemasonry and other secret societies.

The rose is a well-established alchemical symbol of spiritual transformation and the cross is a more familiar symbol of salvation. The Rosicrucians combined these two symbols to represent a gateway of spiritual awareness beyond the physical world.

FAMA FRATERNITATIS

The ideals that are associated with the Rosicrucians were published in 1614 by Lutheran theologian Johann Valentin Andreae in Fama Fraternitatis, *which describes an "invisible college" of "lovers of wisdom" and tells the allegorical story of Christian Rosencreuz (Rosy-cross), a poor medieval German Knight who acquired alchemical secrets in Arabia, then returned to Germany to found the "House of the Holy Spirit" Lodge with eight disciples. They developed a secret language and a written code of conduct:*

1. *To make no public profession of superior knowledge, and to heal the sick free of charge.*
2. *To wear no special garment, but to dress according to the custom of the country in which they lived.*
3. *To return to the House of the Holy Spirit on a certain day each year, for the purpose of mutual help and instruction.*
4. *To seek for a worthy person to succeed each member.*
5. *To adopt the letters R.C. as their sign and mark.*
6. *To keep the existence of the Fraternity a secret for a period of one hundred years.*

According to legend found in Masonic literature, the Rosicrucian order was formed in 46 A.D. from the synthesis of primitive Christianity with Egyptian mysteries after an Alexandrian Gnostic sage named Ormus and his six followers were converted by Mark, one of Jesus' disciples.

Whatever its true origins, one of the aims of the Rosicrucians appears to have been to bring many branches of occultism and alchemy together under one umbrella in the quest for the invisible "spirit" contained in all matter—the scientific quest for a universal theory still underpins modern science today. They earned the name "Fire-Philosophers" along with a reputation for having allegedly discovered the "eternal flame," an obsession among alchemists to rediscover the lost secrets of the ancients' "ever-burning lamps" and connected to the prolonging of life.

Though tiny in membership (in 1623, only thirty-six Rosicrucians were said to be in Europe, scattered about in six different countries), its publications sent shockwaves through the intelligentsia, aristocracy, and scientific communities in Europe, with their quest for spiritual truth and personal enlightenment.

The Rosicrucians' relationship with Freemasonry is difficult to pin down, although prominent figures have been associated with them, many of them also Freemasons: Leonardo da Vinci, Cornelius Heinrich Agrippa, Dante Alighieri, Rene Descartes, Blaise Pascal, Isaac Newton, Gottfried Leibniz, Christopher Wren, Benjamin Franklin (a Rosicrucian colony was established in Philadelphia in the seventeenth century), Thomas Jefferson, Michael Faraday, Claude Debussy, and Erik Satie.

Manly P. Hall highlighted the link in *Lectures on Ancient Philosophy* in 1929: "The outer history of the Masonic order is one of noble endeavor, altruism, and splendid enterprise; the inner history, one of silent conquest, persecution, and heroic martyrdom . . . the Mysteries of Egypt and Persia that had found a haven in the Arabian desert reached Europe by way of the Knights Templars and the Rosicrucians . . . The founders of Freemasonry were all men who were more or less identified with the progressive tendencies of their day. Mystics, philosophers, and alchemists were all bound together with a secret tie and dedicated to the emancipation of humanity from ignorance and oppression."

THE KNIGHTS TEMPLAR

"At least one group of Crusaders brought back more than just heretical hearsay—they reportedly returned to Europe with hard evidence of error and duplicity in church dogma. These Crusaders over time became known as heretics and blasphemers and an attempt was made by the church to exterminate them. They were the Knights Templar, whose traditions live on today within Freemasonry."
—*Jim Marrs,* Rule By Secrecy

At the end of the eleventh century the Middle East was in turmoil. In 1099, the Knights of the First Crusade, led by Godfrey de Bouillon, had captured Jerusalem from the Muslims and created a Christian kingdom, but pilgrims wishing to travel to the Holy Land were far from safe. Nine French crusaders petitioned King Baldwin of Jerusalem and were granted permission to form a religious-military order ostensibly to protect pilgrims. However, their real mission was very different.

Baldwin allowed the knights to live in the east wing of his palace, next to the Al-Aqsa Mosque, built on an ancient site where they believed King Solomon's Temple had stood 2,000 years earlier. The knights became known as the Order of the Poor Knights of Christ and the Temple of Solomon under the leadership of a French nobleman, Hugh de Payens. They immediately began excavating the site, and many researchers believe that they discovered significant artifact: either the Ark of the Covenant, the most sacred Hebrew relic; or, as Graham Hancock believes, powerful secrets ("sacred geometry") and scrolls about the life of Jesus that predate the Gospels and challenge orthodox views about the crucifixion and resurrection. Hancock is convinced that they had "unearthed on the Temple Mount some repository of ancient knowledge concerning the science of building."

Whatever they discovered, it may well have been instrumental in ensuring that during the next two hundred years they would become so powerful that they were second only to the Catholic Church. At the height of their renown, they had 20,000 knights and a fearsome fighting reputation. They were easily recognizable in their white surcoats bearing a red cross.

During their ascendancy they were recognized by the Catholic Church as an official military and religious order, invented the modern banking and credit system *(see page 140)*, held land throughout Europe, and were allowed to build their own churches, until the Order was crushed in 1307 by the pope and the French king.

CHARTRES CATHEDRAL

Along with the Masonic guilds, the Templars became the driving force behind some of the great medieval European churches, most notably Chartres Cathedral in Paris. It seems highly plausible that the Templar's knowledge of sacred geometry accounts for why Chartres Cathedral was so ahead of its time in its design and technology. Its pointed arches and high-vaulted ceilings announced the arrival of early Gothic architecture and even the curious properties of its stained glass still baffle modern chemists.

The Templars adopted a hierarchical structure which they had copied from the Cistercians, which involved reporting to a ruling commander called a Grand Master, and protecting secrets from those Templars who were lower down the chain of command. According to Picknett and Prince, the lower ranks were "simple Christian soldiers, but the inner circle was different." This same criticism has been levelled against the Freemasons time and time again, that the Blue Lodge Masons are ignorant of the real secrets. Some researchers believe their destruction by France's King Philip IV and Pope Clement V was not just because they rivaled the church and monarchy in wealth; it was also rumored that the Templars intended to restore the Merovingian bloodline to the French throne *(see page 100)*. The Merovingians claimed descent from Jesus and were living "proof" that Jesus did not die on the cross. Author Lawrence Gardiner says, "It was widely accepted that the Knights possessed an insight which eclipsed orthodox Christianity, an insight that permitted then the certainty that the Church had misinterpreted both the Virgin Birth and the Resurrection."

In 1314, when the last Templar Grand Master, Jacques de Molay, was burned to death in Paris, the Order met its symbolic, if not literal, end. Many of the Templars fled from France and entered Masonic lodges worldwide. Much of the Templar's vast wealth remains unaccounted for, as does the Templar fleet—one of the largest of the time.

THE BEARDED HEAD

During the Templar heresy trials, many accusations were leveled against them that they worshipped a bearded head. Under torture, many Templars "confessed" to worshipping an idol said to be the Baphomet. There are numerous interpretations of the Baphomet, ranging from the Head of John the Baptist to the Turin Shroud.

It is possible that the Templars had in their possession one of the many heads that were circulating at the time, all of which were alleged to have belonged to John the Baptist. Others have claimed it is a corruption of the word "Mohammed," and that the Templars had adopted this practice in the East, but this is unlikely since the Muslim faith prohibits idolatry, and no such idol existed even in the breakaway sects of the Ismailis or the Druse. As Idries Shah points out in *The Sufis*, Baphomet is more likely to be a "corruption of the Arabic *abufihamat* (pronounced in the Moorish Spanish something like *bufihimat*). The word means 'father of understanding.' In Arabic, 'father' is taken to mean 'source, chief seat of,' and so on. In Sufi terminology, *ras el-fahmat* (head of knowledge) means the mentation of man after undergoing refinement—the transmuted consciousness."

Schonfield showed that by applying the Hebrew Atbash code (numerology) to the name Baphomet, the name Sophia (Shvpia), female wisdom, is revealed. So the Templars venerated Wisdom.

The speculation doesn't end there. Other sources have claimed that the Templars were in possession of the Turin Shroud, and it is this which provides us with the image of the bearded man.

By far, the most intriguing interpretation and one which links the Templars once again to Freemasonry and the Priory of Sion (see below), is that the Baphomet is Asmodeus, the "daemon guardian" whom Solomon summoned to help build his Temple. This same devil supports the font and guards the entrance of the church of Rennes-le-Château, with a bare right shoulder and kneeling on as bare right knee, which bears a striking resemblance to the way a Fellow Craft is dressed during his initiation ritual *(see page 190)*.

Left: Saint John the Baptist. Attributed to artist Meo da Siena

MASONRY, THE PRIORY OF SION, AND THE HOLY GRAIL

According to Picknett and Prince, the Priory of Sion is today a front used by members of the Rectified Scottish Rite and the Martinist Order of Freemasonry, conspiring to restore the Merovingian dynasty to the thrones of Europe.

The secret society is thought to have been established in 1090 by Godfroi de Bouillon, the Duke of Lower Lorraine in France, who had mortgaged his entire inheritance to fund his campaign to the Holy Land. He soon became the overall leader of the successful First Crusade and was proclaimed King of Jerusalem, choosing instead the title, "Guardian of the Sacred Sepulchre."

He had been accompanied by a group of Belgian Monks who believed he was a descendant of the Merovingians, a deposed dynasty of Frankish kings which had ruled over France between the fifth and seventh centuries A.D., only to be overthrown by a rival Carolingian dynasty. However, according to a collection of Priory of Sion documents called the *Dossiers Secrets*, which were discovered in the Bibliothèque Nationale in Paris during the 1960s, the society went underground and survives today.

ALPHA GALATES

The Dossiers Secrets are thought by some sources to be an elaborate hoax, engineered by an extreme right-wing French sect, Alpha Galates, which supposedly invented an ancient lineage and flirted with superficial Masonic and esoteric subjects in order to promote itself and the egos of its anti-Semitic and anti-Masonic organizers—men such as Pierre Plantard, who claimed that he was directly descended from the Merovingian king, Dagobert II. However there are many other strands to this story which link it to Freemasonry.

The society's first base was the Abbey of Our Lady of Mount Sion in Jerusalem, which was built at the order of Godfrey de Bouillon. His knights called themselves the Knights of the Order of Our Lady of Sion and for a while they seem to have had close links with the Knights Templar. Its first Grand Master (or Nautonnier) was a Norman aristocrat called Jean de Gisors, giving rise to a tradition which continues to this day of subsequent Grand Masters adopting the name Jean (or Jeanne for a woman). These have included Botticelli, Leonardo da Vinci, Nostradamus, Isaac Newton, Victor Hugo, Claude Debussy, and Jean Cocteau.

The place which is the present-day focus for researchers wishing to uncover the origins and secrets of the Priory of Sion is the small hilltop Catholic church of St. Mary Magdalene, in the tiny parish of Rennes-le-Château in the Languedoc region of France. In 1891, while restoring the church, a thirty-three-year-old priest, François Bérenger Saunière discovered secret documents which dramatically changed his fortunes, leading many to suspect that he was paid to keep quiet.

Some accounts claim he found a secret parchment inside one of the altar supports; other sources claim he discovered two genealogies dating from the thirteenth and seventeenth centuries and two encrypted messages in the graveyard outside on the tombstone of Marie de Nègre d'Ables, Lady of Blanchfort and widow of the last Lord of Rennes-le-Château, who had died in 1781.

He immediately sought advice from his superior, the Bishop at Carcassonne, who packed him off to Paris to the Saint Sulpice Seminary, which has been described as the headquarters of a secret society called the Compagnie du Saint-Sacrement, an early incarnation of the Priory of Sion. Upon his return he received large sums of money to refurbish his church and adopted an opulent and dissolute lifestyle with his new found wealth. He is also reputed to have conducted an indiscrete affair with a Parisian Opera singer and occultist, Emma Calve.

He commissioned a statue of Asmodeus, the "daemon guardian," whom Solomon summoned to help build his Temple (*see page 15*) and built a painted panel with an ambiguous depiction of the body of Jesus being secretly removed from his tomb. However, his renovations weren't limited to the church. His benefactors paid for the building of a large library, a zoological garden, and the Tour Magdala (dedicated to Mary Magdalene, the woman whom the Merovingians claimed founded its dynasty by fathering Jesus's children).

French author Gérard de Sède believes that the ninth station of the cross alludes to a Masonic order known as the Beneficent Knight of the Holy City; also, that the noble families of Rennes-le-Château were senior figures in the Rectified Scottish Rite of Masonry. Whatever he discovered he took with him to his grave, but the many clues in the form of Masonic symbols which he left in his church are a strong indication that his good fortune was Masonic.

Saunière clearly discovered powerful information. Some sources believe he uncovered proof that Jesus did not die on the cross, but lived to father the Merovingian dynasty with Mary Magdalene, and that the Holy Grail or Sangreal of Arthurian legend wasn't an artefact, the legendary sacred vessel associated with divine revelation, whose origins go back to the Last Supper, but a bloodline—the Sang Real—that lives on in the Merovingian dynasty, kept alive and protected by the Masonic Priory of Sion.

Right: Sir Perceval and the Holy Grail

Saint-Sulpice by Rouargue Freres. Saint-Sulpice was allegedly the headquarters of an earlier incarnation of the Priory of Sion

George Washington
(1732–1799)

Initiated 1752, Fredericksburg Lodge No. 4, Virginia

In 1784, he received a white satin Holy Royal Arch Masonic apron from Gilbert Lafayette, French aristocrat and a powerful influence in the French Revolution. In 1788, Washington was appointed Worshipful Master of Alexandria Lodge No. 22, Virginia.

In 1797, he addressed the Grand Lodge of Massachusetts: "My attachment to the Society of which we are all members will dispose me always to contribute my best endeavors to promote the honor and prosperity of the Craft." According to General Lafayette, his ties lay much deeper. Washington "never willingly gave independent command to officers who were not Freemasons. Nearly all the members of his official family, as well as most other officers who shared his inmost confidence, were his brethren of the mystic tie."

 Famous Freemasons Past and Present

Duke of Wellington
(1769–1852)

Initiated 1790, Lodge at Trim No. 494, Meath, Ireland

His father and brothers were Masters of the same lodge, but after joining he never attended another meeting.

In 1838, a lodge in Dublin wanted to change its name to Wellington Lodge, so they wrote him a letter asking for his blessing. The letter that Wellington wrote in response leaves no doubt that he wished to distance himself from the Craft: "The Duke of Wellington presents his compliments to Mr. Carleton. He perfectly recollects that he was admitted to the lowest grade of Free Masonry in a lodge which was formed at Trim in the County of Meath. He has never since attended a lodge of Free Masons . . . [naming the Lodge after him] would be a ridiculous assumption of the reputation of being attached to Free Masonry, in addition to being a misrepresentation."

 Famous Freemasons Past and Present

CHAPTER 7
Masonic Murder

Conspiracy theories involving Freemasonry are nothing new. They have been in circulation since as far back as the late eighteenth century when a French priest, Abbe Augustin Barruel, a refugee in London after the French Revolution, wrote his *Memoirs of the History of Jacobinism and Freemasonry*. Since then, Freemasonry has been linked to the deaths of many famous people, including Amadeus Mozart and William Morgan. Even the murders of Jack the Ripper have been blamed on a Masonic conspiracy.

AMADEUS MOZART

Mozart died a swift, though agonizing death at the age of thirty-five in the early hours of December 5, 1791. During his short life he had composed over 600 compositions, many of which are considered the greatest musical achievements the world has ever heard. He had never enjoyed good health. As a child he had suffered from endless maladies, and in adulthood his health was compromised by excessive drinking, venereal diseases, poverty, rheumatism, fast living, and overwork.

However, his "sudden" death came as a great shock to his admirers, and rumors began to circulate that he had been poisoned. His widow, Constanze, claimed that Mozart himself suspected that someone had poisoned him, and that was why he felt the urgent need to finish his *Requiem Mass* on his deathbed, so that it could be played at his funeral.

The official cause of death was "severe miliary fever," a description that is so ambiguous that it reveals that the doctors didn't have the first clue what killed him. The most likely explanation is that a variety of complications caused his death, but he was barely cold in his pauper's grave before speculation was directed towards the Freemasons, whom it was rumored killed him for revealing Masonic secrets in "The Magic Flute" (*see page 70*).

One Mozart expert says, "If murder had occurred there were certainly many suspects, he owed a great deal of money to a wide cross section of Viennese society and made many enemies at the Imperial Court. He was also a notorious womanizer." There was no shortage of people with a motive for murder.

Mozart may indeed have been poisoned, but on the advice of his ignorant doctors. According to some sources Mozart was instructed to drink "acqua toffana," which was a remedy for stomach diseases. This "medicine" consists of water, bitter salts, and arsenic.

THE MORGAN AFFAIR

The Morgan Affair still haunts modern Masonry today and remains a sobering reminder that public opinion needs few excuses to point an accusatory finger.

William Morgan was an opportunist and alleged Freemason who disappeared in 1826 after attempting to publish Masonic secrets. Since then, many explanations have been put forward to account for the events, the most common being that Morgan was murdered by Masons. "The Morgan Affair," as it became known, set off an anti-Masonic backlash which would lead to the closure of many lodges and the formation of the Anti-Masonic Political Party, enlisting among its leaders John Quincy Adams.

William Morgan lived in Batavia, New York, from 1824 to 1826. Accounts of him differ, but he seems to have been a man of questionable character, a heavy drinker who neglected his family, and was frequently in debt. He quite probably gained admission to local Masonic lodges under false pretences. He attended lodge meetings, made speeches, and frequently benefited from Masonic charity. Suspicions began to grow about his conduct and Masonic credentials, since his name was omitted from membership rolls when a new Charter was granted. He became embittered and struck up a publishing deal with David C. Miller, a disgraced Mason and editor of the *Republican Advocate*, a weekly local newspaper.

Morgan boasted publicly about how much money he was going to make from exposing Masonic secrets and stirred up much resentment among the Masonic fraternity, which contrived to have him arrested for bad debts (amounting to $2.68) and jailed. One day later, his bail was paid and he was last seen being escorted out of the town in the company of several men.

There are three explanations for what happened next. The anti-Masonic version states that he was abducted and taken a hundred and twenty five miles to Fort Niagara, where he was killed. Masons Nicholas Chesebro, Loton Lawson, and Edward Sawyer pleaded guilty to conspiracy to "seize and secrete" Morgan. These three, along with Sheriff Eli Bruce and John Whitney, went to prison for the offense. But murder was never proved because his body was never recovered. The second explanation is that he was paid a large sum of money by Freemasons to disappear into Canada and never return. The third explanation is that Morgan simply escaped, with or without a pay-off, abandoning his family.

The Morgan Affair led to Masons being attacked in the streets, their property vandalized, business relations severed, and mock lodge meetings conducted in public to expose Masonic secrets. Thousands of Masons resigned from the brotherhood and many lodges ceased to exist. Within a decade the number of Masons in the U.S. fell from around 100,000 to 40,000, and in New York state numbers fell from 20,000 to under 3,000 and over 400 lodges closed.

Whatever the truth, William Morgan's disappearance has been held up as an example of Masonic evil-doing ever since.

JACK THE RIPPER

"Jack the Ripper is a misnomer. The name conjures up visions of a lone assassin, stalking his victims under the foggy gaslight of Whitechapel. It is just this mistaken notion, inspired almost solely by that terrifying nickname, which rendered the murders of five East End prostitutes in 1888 insoluble. For Jack the Ripper was not one man, but three, two killers and an accomplice. The facts surrounding their exploits have never before been teased from the confused skeins of truths, half-truths and lies which have been woven around this case."

—*Stephen Knight,* Jack the Ripper: The Final Solution

Author Stephen Knight makes a case that the murders of five East End prostitutes within the space of nine weeks in 1888 were the result of a Masonic plot, involving Sir William Gull, the Queen's physician, and Sir Charles Warren, Commissioner of Police and Grand Master of the Ars Quator Coronatorum Masonic Lodge. They hatched the plot to protect the Monarchy and prevent a royal secret from becoming a public scandal.

Knight argues that Queen Victoria's bisexual grandson, "Prince Eddy," had fathered a child with a young Roman Catholic shop girl, Annie Crook. He was associating with the artist Walter Sickert at the time, who introduced them. Sickert arranged for a woman named Mary Kelly to become the illegitimate child's nanny, but she attempted to blackmail the Crown along with three of the other victims.

Knight highlights numerous circumstances about the murders which make a convincing case for them being contract killings rather than the random butchery of a diseased maniac. There were about 100,000 prostitutes in London at the time and yet all of the victims knew each other and socialized together. This cannot be explained simply by the fact that the murders happened in the same vicinity—they didn't. The bodies were found miles apart, despite the fact that they all lived on the same street; the chances of this would be very slim if these were random killings.

Mary Kelly was the fifth and final victim, but the fourth victim also used the street name Mary Kelly, which suggests that she was killed in error. Again, this is a coincidence too great to be ignored.

The way in which the bodies were mutilated points to Masonic ritual. The murderer or murderers left clues that are unequivocal for those familiar with Masonic practices.

All the bodies had their throat cut across (the punishment for Entered Apprentices who reveal Masonic secrets—*see page 56*). The second victim, Annie Chapman, was disemboweled and her small intestines were placed above her right shoulder, while her stomach was placed above her left shoulder. Her jewelry and coins were removed and two brass rings were placed at her feet (a candidate is prepared for the second degree of freemasonry by having all metal items removed from his person—*see page 190*). On a wall above the third victim, Elizabeth Stride, the killer wrote, "The Juwes are the men that will not be blamed for nothing." "Juwes" is the collective name for the "three ruffians" (as they are known today) who murdered Hiram Abiff (*see page 15*). This slogan was immediately erased upon the orders of police official Sir Charles Warren, despite protests from others in the police force who wanted to preserve this vital evidence. The body of Catherine Eddowes (alias Mary Kelly) was found in Mitre Square. The mitre and square are important Masonic symbols (*see page 48*). Her face and other parts of her body had been mutilated using triangular cuts. The fifth victim was killed in her apartment, and it is likely that some of her internal organs were "burned to ashes" in the fireplace, a reference to the punishment in the third degree (*see page 62*).

The most disturbing symbol of all is revealed when the five murder sites are viewed on a map. They can be joined up to form the demonic "Goathead" pentagram, also known as the Sigl of Baphomet. This Masonic symbol also appears in street layout of Washington, D.C. (*see page 161*).

According to Knight, Gull arranged for Annie Crook to be committed to an insane asylum where he performed experiments on her and cut out parts of her brain to erase her memories.

Counter-arguments highlight several inconsistencies, namely that the illegitimate child was conceived at a time when Prince Eddy was in Heidelberg, Germany, and Annie Crook was in London. Dr. Gull, the man alleged to have been behind, and even responsible, for the murders was a frail man of seventy-two who had already suffered a stroke and a heart attack. Finally, the building where Knight alleges an illicit liaison took place had been demolished two years earlier. No doubt this conspiracy theory will endure for a long time to come.

President McKinley being honored by Freemasons

Oscar Wilde (1854–1900)

Initiated 1875, Apollo University Lodge No. 357, Oxford, England

He joined the Masons three years before he moved to London with the express purpose of achieving superstardom. Although many claim that Freemasons corrupt the judicial system to protect their Brothers, it didn't seem to keep Wilde out of jail for sodomy twenty years later.

 Famous Freemasons Past and Present

Christopher Wren
(1632–1723)

Initiated 1691, Lodge of Antiquity No. 2, London, England

As Surveyor of the King's Works, architect of St. Paul's Cathedral, and president of the Royal Society, there is no shortage of documents, letters, and drawings relating to his life and his professional activities, but there is no mention in any of these documents to his being a Freemason, nor did he keep a diary.

The only evidence that the great man was a Freemason can be found in a handwritten note added to the manuscript of John Aubrey's *Naturall Historie of Wiltshire* in 1685, which is kept in the Bodleian library at Oxford: "MDM, this day (May 1691 the 18th, being Monday after Rogation Sunday) is a great convention at St. Pauls' church of the Fraternity of the Accepted . . . masons where Sir Christopher Wren is to be adopted a Brother: and Sir Henry Goodric of ye tower, & divers . . . others—and there have been kings, that have been of this -Sodalitie."

Many people see this as evidence enough that he was indeed a member, although John Hamill, in his 1986 book *The Craft*, says it is plausible, but "it is not proven."

Wren was a founding member of the Royal Society, which was granted its Royal Charter by Charles II in October 1662. Several other prominent members of the Royal Society were Freemasons, such as Sir Robert Moray and the philosopher and theorist of liberalism, John Locke, who admitted to being a Freemason in a letter dated 1696. What is surprising is that Wren waited until he was almost sixty years old before becoming a Freemason, since its enlightenment values ought to have attracted him much sooner.

 Famous Freemasons Past and Present

CHAPTER 8
Secrets and Lies

Revolution and war have always been the most direct and extreme forces of change in society. During the last few centuries Freemasonry has been quick to foment and exploit revolutionary tensions and to profit from the consequences of civil or international strife. It is only with hindsight that this influence can be so clearly revealed; only time will allow us to see how contemporary Masonic schemes will play out in the future, although many already believe that the introduction of the EURO *(see page 146)* has been instrumental in furthering the Masonic agenda.

The creation of wealth through conflict is a recurrent theme in the history of the Brotherhood, and the events which precipitated World War I *(see page 136)* are shining examples of behind-the-scenes Masonic power struggles.

Masonic symbolism has been indelibly stamped into prominent features of American and European society, from the design of currencies to the obelisks and architecture that have shaped entire cities.

REVOLUTION: HOW FREEMASONS PLOTTED THE REVOLUTIONS IN FRANCE, AMERICA, AND RUSSIA.

"If one desires to point to a major world event proven to have been inspired by secret society machinations, one need look no further than the French Revolution."

—*Jim Marrs,* Rule by Secrecy

The French Revolution was the pivotal event of European history in the eighteenth century. From its start in 1789, it transformed social values and political systems in France and the rest of Europe, and eventually throughout the world. The revolutionary leaders wanted individual liberty, constitutional government, elections, and civil equality for all. They rose up against the corrupt and decadent court of King Louis XVI and his queen, Marie Antoinette, yet his regime was no more tyrannical or unjust than those which had preceded him. So what was the catalyst which set off this revolutionary upheaval? It looks increasingly likely that is was the Freemasons.

The most famous claim that the Masons were responsible for the French Revolution was made by the alchemist and Freemason, Count Cagliostro. He was a favorite of the King and the French court at Versailles and he revealed that Masons throughout Europe had been planning a chain of revolutions with the aim of destroying the Papacy or to take it over. This is tantalizing evidence but we must look for further proof, since he made these claims while being tortured by the Spanish Inquisition.

Scholars are now beginning to revisit the analysis of Nesta H. Webster, who wrote in 1924, "The Masons . . . originated the Revolution with the infamous Duke of Orleans at their head." The causes of the French Revolution are many and deep rooted, but it had previously been widely believed that it was fomented by lack of food and government representation. However, in *The French Revolution* (1919), Webster wrote, "The lodges of the German Freemasons and Illuminati were thus the source whence emanated all those

anarchic schemes which culminated in the Terror, and it was at a great meeting of the Freemasons in Frankfurt-am-Main, three years before the French Revolution began, that the deaths of Louis XVI and Gustavus III of Sweden were first planned."

Jean-Joseph Mounier provides an argument which appears to refute this. He was an eye-witness and participated in the Revolution (he proposed the Tennis Court Oath—that the assertion that sovereignty of the people did not reside in the King, but in the people themselves). In his book, *On the Influence Attributed to Philosophers, Freemasons, and to the Illuminati on the Revolution of France*, Mounier says, "Among the noble conspirators who prepared the death of Gustavus, I do not know a single one who has been desirous of playing a part in the Revolution of France, although this would have been extremely easy for them." Mournier insists that neither the philosophes (an enlightened group of French thinkers who thrived in the middle of the eighteenth century), nor the Freemasons, nor the Illuminati had any hand in the uprising.

Nesta H. Webster counters his view by pointing out that Mounier wrote his book in Germany and collected his information from Johann Joachim Christoph Bode, a prominent Mason and reputed to have been the head of the Illuminati. It seems that the Illuminati's covert power was such that they managed to convince prominent men of letters to cover their tracks!

The main arguments that scholars use to connect the Masons with the Revolution are that the Duke of Orleans was a Grand Master of French Masonry (according to Jim Marrs, "It was the Duke of Orleans . . . who reportedly bought all the grain in 1789 and either sold it abroad or hid it away, thus creating near starvation among the commoners."); that Marquis de Lafayette, the man who had been initiated into the Masonic fraternity by George Washington, also played an important role in the French revolutionary cause; and finally, that the Jacobin Club, the radical nucleus of the French revolutionary movement was founded by prominent Freemasons and the network of other Jacobin clubs copied the organizational structure of Freemasons.

Left: Duke of Orleans

Historian George Armstrong Kelly doesn't believe that the Duke of Orleans instigated the French people to rebellion by depriving them of food. He says, "The harsh winter, crop failures, and an alarming ascent of prices from 1785 on accounted for that."

However, as alternative historian Richard Fusniak points out, you only have to look at revolutionary celebrations to see a Masonic connection: "The first celebrations of the French Revolution that took place in 1793 saw many makeshift 'pyramids' raised in the heart of Paris and in the courtyard of the Louvre Museum, causing many historians to suspect a Masonic involvement. Today, a glass pyramid with the same geometrical pro-portions as the Great Pyramid of Giza adorns the courtyard of the Louvre."

Masonry's mission in France did not stop with the revolution. It continued through the reign of the Emperor Napoleon, a Freemason. Some conspiracy theorists believe that after the Revolution, all the anti-clerical measures passed in the French Parliament were decreed beforehand in the Masonic lodges and that all the "anti-clerical" reforms carried out in France since 1877, such as the secularization of education, measures against pri-vate Christian schools and charitable establishments were part of the ongoing Masonic plot to secularize society.

In this context, the *Catholic Encyclopedia* talks about "an anti-Christian and irreligious reorganization of human society, not only in France but throughout the world. Thus French Freemasonry, as the standard-bearer of all Freemasonry, pretends to inaugurate the golden era of the Masonic universal republic, comprising in Masonic brotherhood all men and all nations."

Some believe this agenda is still being carried out today. Freemasons may have succeeded in the removal of Catholicism as the official religion of France in 1881. As recently as 1988 religious education was completely removed from the education system in France, thanks to (as some believe) the ongoing agenda of Freemasonry to create an anti-Christian and secular reorganization of human society, not only in France but throughout the world.

Right: Commemoration of the Storming of the Bastille

THE AMERICAN REVOLUTION

"It would be difficult to exaggerate the importance of Masonry for the American Revolution. It not only created national icons that are still with us; it brought people together in new ways and helped fulfill the republican dream of reorganizing social relationships. For thousands of Americans, it was a major means by which they participated directly in the Enlightenment . . . Many of the revolutionary leaders, including Washington, Franklin, Samuel Adams, Otis, Richard Henry Lee, Madison, and Hamilton, were members of the fraternity."
—*Gordon S. Wood,* The Radicalism of the American Revolution

It is more than a mere revisionist delusion of American Freemasons that Freemasonry played a pivotal role in the American Revolution. Bernard Fay, a French historian, is convinced that Freemasonry was the "main instigator of the intellectual revolution" of the Enlightenment and "the spiritual father of its political revolutions." He argues that Freemasons engendered among "a limited but very prominent class of people a feeling of American unity without which American liberty could not have developed—without which there would have been no United States."

Masonic author Sidney Morse sets out a case for Freemasons being responsible for angry colonists' burning of the British schooner *Gaspee* in 1772, and following the Masonic-led Boston Tea Party they dominated the Continental Congress (the legislative assembly composed of delegates from the rebel colonies which issued the Declaration of Independence and framed the Articles of Confederation). Furthermore, he wrote that the Freemason George Washington, "according to La Fayette, it is said, never willingly gave independent command to officers who were not Freemasons." Little wonder then that the George Washington National Memorial was funded entirely with voluntary contributions from members of the Masonic Fraternity. Its construction has been descibed by Masonic sources as "the only unified effort of all of the Grand Lodges in the

Right: Lithograph After Spirit of '76 *by Archibald M. Willard*

United States." However, Neil L. York believes that the case has been overstated, made worse he says by the fact that "Masonic lodges left skimpy records, and Masons rarely mentioned such ties in their correspondence. More vexing still for the historian, they virtually never linked their Masonic association to their political views."

Freemasonry is a secret society which works by bringing men and their ideas together in active participation. Masons such as George Washington, Benjamin Franklin, Paul Revere, John Paul Jones, the Marquis de Lafayette, Henry Knox, Joseph Warren, Baron Von Steuben, and Richard Montgomery surely didn't have to leave a paper trail in order achieve their revolutionary goals.

THE BOSTON TEA PARTY

On the evening of December 16, 1773, a group of men calling themselves the "Sons of Liberty" boarded three British ships, and threw forty-five tons of tea into the Boston Harbor. Most Americans today have heard of the Boston Tea Party. Few are aware that nearly all of these agitators were Freemasons, and that those that weren't joined up shortly afterwards.

That single act was the culmination of several years of harsh taxation from Britain, which wanted to reduce its enormous national debt, and recoup the cost of protecting the colonies from the French. Its repercussions were felt up and down the east coast of America, as other seaports staged similar acts of resistance.

Before the War of Independence there were thirteen British colonies in North America, but the government's failure to recognize that they were ready for self-government, coupled with the resented taxation without representation, proved the tipping point. In the preceeding years, the Crown had introduced a series of measures designed to increase the powers of the British Customs officials, and in 1765 the Stamp Act had introduced the first directly imposed taxation. It was repealed the following year, but was followed by the Townshend Acts which imposed duties on a wide range of goods including glass, lead, paper, and tea. This, too, was repealed five years later, after rioting in Boston resulted in the deaths of five men, but the levy remained on tea.

However, the Masonic Sons of Liberty had other plans. They made life a living hell for Customs officials. The final straw came when the British government gave the British East India Company a monopoly to sell tea to the colonies without paying duty, so that it could undercut the price of smuggled tea. It figured that the colonists would leap at the chance to buy cheap tea legally rather than on the black market. However, the powerful merchants in New York, Philadelphia, and Charleston canceled their orders, leaving only the Boston merchants digging their heels in.

Right: Crates of tea are ditched from the Dartmouth *in Boston Harbor*

When three British ships—the *Beaver*, the *Eleanor*, and the *Dartmouth*—sailed into Boston Harbor at the end of November 1773, the Sons of Liberty were waiting to prevent them from unloading. The ships were refused permission by the Customs officials to sail out of the harbor and the scene looked set for a stalemate, ending in the tea being forfeited. However, the Masons of the Boston Lodge of St. Andrew had already hatched a plot which would change the course of American and British history.

According to Sven G. Lunden in *The American Mercury*, "it is no secret that the 'Indians' who dumped the cargo on December 16, 1773, had emerged from the building which housed the St. Andrews Lodge, the leading Masonic body in Boston. Their job done, the 'Indians' were seen to troop back to the lodge building—and no Indians ever again emerged from the lodge. Instead, a lot of prominent Bostonians, known to be Masons, did emerge."

During the late eighteenth century, the Lodge of St. Andrew was very busy and the Minute book shows that it was the hub of much Masonic activity. However, on December 16, the record simply shows a blank page with a letter "T." The lodge was closed that night. Whether or not the letter refers to tea is unclear, but the lodge was undeniably closed on that fateful Thursday evening—stark proof that its members may have been gainfully employed elsewhere. The fight for independence had begun.

Simón Bolívar and the Liberation of South America

In the history of South America, the achievements of one man stand out above all the rest. During, his lifetime he succeeded in liberating northern South America and became known as The Liberator. His name was Simón Bolívar.

The fact that this great leader was also a Freemason may not seem very significant today, were it not for a key moment in his campaign when, as many Masonic and non-Masonic commentators believe, he used his Masonic credentials to change the course of South American history.

He was born on July 24, 1783, in Caracas, Venezuela into an aristocratic family. He enjoyed a very good private education and received tuition from the great intellectuals Andrés Bello and Simón Rodríguez. In 1799 he went to Spain to continue his education, where he met his future wife; after she died he traveled to France in 1804, where he was present at the crowning of Napoleon as emperor. He then continued to Rome, where he vowed to liberate South America from the Spanish.

He then traveled to Paris, where he was introduced to Freemasonry, and he was initiated into the Scottish Rite when he returned to Venezuela in 1807.

When Napoleon invaded Spain and installed his older brother, Joseph Bonaparte, as king, the South American colonies set up a *junta* which refused to recognize his sovereignty. Bolívar, who had become a lieutenant colonel under the *junta*, took part in the liberation of Caracas and the subsequent declaration of Venezuelan independence in June 1811. After a counter-rebellion, Bolívar fled to New Granada (present-day Colombia), where he persuaded the Colombians to unite with their neighbors to free Venezuela. He then installed himself as dictator of Venezuela, until he was again forced to flee, this time to Jamaica, after being defeated by José Tomás Boves.

Bolívar lobbied for support in Haiti, then returned to South America to continue the struggle for independence. As his success and popularity grew, he retook Venezuela and later became the first president of Gran Colombia.

What happened next remains a mystery to this day, and some see it as proof of the mysterious power of Freemasonry. Bolívar wanted to free Peru, so he arranged a secret meeting with the great liberator of Chile and Argentina, José de San Martin. It is thought that at this meeting Bolívar pulled Masonic rank over Martin (who was also a Mason). Martin subsequently resigned as president of Argentina and stepped aside so that Bolívar could claim the glory of liberating Peru. He succeeded, and upper Peru was name Bolivia in his honor.

The Russian Revolution

"There indeed exists a wealth of documentation indicating that the Russian Revolution—indeed the very creation of Communism—sprang from Western conspiracies beginning even before World War I."
—*Jim Marrs,* Rule by Secrecy

One of the main objections raised against the idea that the Russian Revolution was engineered and bankrolled by wealthy British, German, and American financiers is the apparent absurdity of creating a political movement which aimed to strip the wealthy of their fortunes. Revolutionary Saul Alinsky attributes it to pure greed: "As for businessmen, I could persuade a capitalist on Friday to bankroll a revolution on Saturday that will bring him a profit on Sunday even though he will be executed on Monday."

Russian leader Vladimir Ilyich Lenin wanted to exploit this greed, apparently making him a player rather than pawn: "The Capitalists of the world and their governments, in pursuit of conquest of the Soviet market, will close their eyes to the indicated higher reality and thus will turn into deaf mute blindmen. They will extend credits, which will strengthen for us the Communist Party in their countries, and giving us the materials and technology we lack, they will restore our military industry, indispensable for our future victorious attacks on our suppliers. In other words, they will labor for the preparation for their own suicide."

Gary Allen, author of the 1971 underground classic, *None Dare Call It Conspiracy*, explains the paradox from a different perspective: "Obviously these men [Rothschilds, Rockefellers, Schiffs, Warburgs, Morgans, Harrimans and Milners] have no fear of international communism. It is only logical to assume that if they financed it and do not fear it, it must be because they control it. Can there be any other explanation that makes sense?"

The real reason that the bankers were prepared to support an ideology which threatened their position was that secret societies, the Freemasons included, had successfully used the powerful principle of dialectic—the attempt to reconcile opposites—for centuries, even before the German philosopher Georg Wilhelm Friedrich Hegel and revolutionary

Above: Leon Trotsky

Karl Marx made it their own. Hegel may have rationalized the Hegelian System, but the man who most influenced his work was a Freemason named Johann Gottlieb Fichte. "The members of secret societies . . . had found it [Hegelian dialectic] was but a small step to the realization that one needn't wait for crisis and turmoil. Social upheaval could be created and controlled to their own benefit. Hence came the cycles of financial booms and busts, crises and revolutions, wars and threats of wars, all of which maintained a balance of power."

In 1917, Leon Trotsky was living in New York, where he met with several wealthy Wall Street bankers (including Freemasons Jacob Schiff, Elihu Root, and Lord Alfred Milner) who were more than willing to finance a revolution in Russia. According to David Icke, two years earlier the "American International Corporation was formed to fund the Russian Revolution. Its directors represented the interests of the Rockefeller, Rothschilds, Du Pont, Kuhn, Loeb, Harriman, and the Federal Reserve." In March he set off in a ship with 275 revolutionaries and enormous amounts of funding with the stated intention of "going back to Russia to overthrow the provisional government and stop the war with Germany." He was almost immediately stopped at Halifax, Nova Scotia, but was released on the instruction of Woodrow Wilson and Colonel House. He was given an American passport and was waved on to Russia.

Meanwhile, Lenin left his exile in Switzerland and embarked on a sealed train with at least $5 million in gold. He traveled through Germany without being challenged, thanks to the arrangements of Freemason and Illuminati banker Max Warburg and the German High Command. The rest is history, even if the ideals of the revolution and its legacy didn't go quite as planned.

THE SPOILS OF WAR

The ruling classes, operating within secret societies such as the Illuminati, Freemasons, and the Council on Foreign Relations, have throughout history conspired to bring about war, so that they can profit from lending money to both sides. World War I is a prime example of this.

Most people wrongly believe that the war was caused by the assassination of Archduke Francis (Franz) Ferdinand of Austria-Hungary in 1914. The real cause was Masonic powerbrokers, who made millions from the ensuing carnage. Edward Griffin calls this the "Rothschild Formula," which he says has controlled the political climate of Europe since the late eighteenth century. Furthermore, he states that "an arms race had been in progress for many years . . . The assassination of Ferdinand was not the cause but the trigger."

Jim Marrs pins the blame squarely on the Freemasons: "According to a 1952 Masonic publication, Ferdinand's assassin, the Bosnian Serb Gavrilo Princip, and others were Freemasons, encouraged by Apis [Colonel Dragutin Dimitrijevic, chief of Serbian military intelligence] and incensed by disclosure of a secret treaty between the Vatican and Serbia. The Death of Ferdinand caused a chain reaction of ultimatums and mobilizations which ultimately spread war from the Balkans to the whole of Europe."

However, the war would not have been the economic opportunity it became if the Americans had not been persuaded to join in. In 1909 the Carnegie Endowment for International Peace had concluded after a year of discussions that, "There are no known means more efficient than war, assuming the objective is altering the life of an entire people." They then posed themselves a question: "How do we involve the United States in a war?"

This was no mean feat, since the U.S. had always been very keen to follow the advice of George Washington "to steer clear of permanent alliance with any portion of the foreign world." Just five months before the Americans joined the war, Woodrow Wilson had been re-elected to the Presidency on an isolationist anti-war ticket. So what was it that caused such an abrupt about face?

Right: The New York Times reports the assassination of Archduke Franz Ferdinand

THE WEATHER

Local showers today; Tuesday, fair; fresh, shifting winds, becoming northwest.

☞For full weather report see Page 17.

NE 29, 1914.—EIGHTEEN PAGES.　　　ONE CENT　In Greater New York, Jersey City and Newark.　Elsew TWO CE

HEIR TO AUSTRIA'S THRONE IS SLAIN WITH HIS WIFE BY A BOSNIAN YOUTH TO AVENGE SEIZURE OF HIS COUNTR

Francis Ferdinand Shot During State Visit to Sarajevo.

TWO ATTACKS IN A DAY

Archduke Saves His Life First Time by Knocking Aside a Bomb Hurled at Auto.

SLAIN IN SECOND ATTEMPT

Lad Dashes at Car as the Royal Couple Return from Town Hall and Kills Both of Them.

LAID TO A SERVIAN PLOT

Heir Warned Not to Go to Bosnia, Where Populace Met Him with Servian Flags.

AGED EMPEROR IS STRICKEN

Shock of Tragedy Prostrates Francis Joseph—Young Assassin Proud of His Crime.

Special Cable to THE NEW YORK TIMES.

SARAJEVO, Bosnia, June 28, (By courtesy of the Vienna Neue Freie Presse.)—Archduke Francis Ferdinand, **heir** to the throne of Austria-Hungary, and his wife, the Duchess of Hohenberg, were shot and killed by a Bosnian student here today. The fatal shooting was the second attempt upon the lives of the couple during the day, and is believed to have been the result of a political conspiracy.

This morning, as Archduke Francis Ferdinand and the Duchess were driving to a reception at the Town Hall a bomb was thrown at their motor car. The Archduke pushed it off with his arm.

The bomb did not explode until after the Archduke's car had passed

Archduke Francis Ferdinand and his Consort, the Duchess of Hohent

Slain by Assassin's Bullets.

could only certify they were both dead.

The authors of both attacks upon the Archduke are born Bosnians. Gabrinovics is a compositor, and worked for a few weeks in the Government printing works at Belgrade. He returned to Sarajevo a Servian chauvinist, and made no concealment of his sympathies with the King of Servia. Both he and the actual murderer of the Archduke and the Duchess expressed themselves to the police in the most cynical fashion about their crimes.

ARCHDUKE IGNORED WARNING.

Servian Minister Feared Trouble if Heir Went to Bosnia.

Special Cable to THE NEW YORK TIMES.

VIENNA, June 28.—When the news of the assassination of the Archduke Francis Ferdinand and the Duchess was broken to the aged Emperor Francis Joseph he said: "Horrible, horrible! No sorrow is spared me."

The Emperor, who yesterday left here for Ischl, his favorite Summer resort, amid acclamations of the people, will return to Vienna at once, in spite of the hardships of the journey in the terrible heat.

by splinters from the bomb. Several persons on the pavement were very seriously hurt by the explosion of the bomb, which was thrown by a young man named Tabrinovitch, (Gabrinovics,) who is a typist from Trebenje, in Herzegovina, and is of Servian nationality. He was arrested some twenty minutes later.

The Archduke and his wife left the Town Hall, intending to visit those who had been injured by the bomb, when a schoolboy 19 years old, named Prinzip, who came from Grahovo, fired a shot at the Archduke's head. The boy fired from the shelter of a projecting house.

Wore Bullet-Proof Coat.

The boy must have been carefully instructed in his part, for it was a well-guarded secret that the Archduke always wore a coat of silk strands which were woven obliquely, so that no weapon or bullet could pierce it. I once saw a strip of this fabric used for a motor-car tire, and it was puncture-proof. This new invention enabled the Archduke to brave attempts on his life, but his head naturally was uncovered.

The Duchess was shot in the body. The boy fired several times, but only two shots took effect. The Archduke and his wife were carried to the Konak, or palace, in a dying condition. Later details show that the assassin darted forth from his hiding place behind a house and actually got on the

it is feared that it will lead to s complications with that unruly dom, and may have far-reachir sults. The future of the empir subject of general discussion. felt that the Servians have treated too leniently, and some words are being said about the ent foreign policy.

All the public buildings are d in long black streamers and the are all at half-mast.

BRAVERY OF ARCHDUK

Gave First Aid to Those W by the Bomb.

SARAJEVO, Bosnia, June 28.—duke Francis Ferdinand, heir Austro-Hungarian throne, and Duchess of Hohenberg, his mor wife, were shot dead in the main of the Bosnian capital by a student while they were making an triumphal progress through the on their annual visit to the a provinces of Bosnia and Herzego

The Archduke was hit full in and the Duchess was shot throu abdomen and throat. Their w proved fatal within a few minu ter they reached the palace. they were hurried with all speed

Those responsible for the ass tion took care that it would pr fective, as there were two assa the first armed with a bomb other with a revolver. The bom thrown at the royal automobile was proceeding to the Town Hall a reception was to be held, t

Wilson became President because of the backing of Masonic bankers J. P. Morgan, Bernard Baruch, Jacob Schiff, and Cleveland Dodge. During the war, Morgan "oversaw the transfer of tremendous amounts of money as the war continued. He bought more than $3 billion in American military and other materials on behalf of the Allied powers while organizing more than two thousand U.S. banks to underwrite more than $1.5 billion in Allied bonds." The bonanza continued after the war, when Morgan's firm "arranged loans totalling more than $10 billion to reconstruct the European nations." Wilson appointed Baruch head of the War Industries Board, where he oversaw all domestic war material contracts, making over $200 million himself. In short, Wilson's genuine desire to keep America out of the war was in direct conflict with the interests of the men who put him in office.

Before America joined the war, everything was going wrong. Germany appeared to be winning, and the Masonic money men would have been ruined. However, the American public had to be given a very good reason to join in, and they were very resistant. So the Rockefeller-Morgan controlled media-propaganda machine rumbled into action, and any publications which were not within its control were "intimidated by the strength of [their] advertising dollars." Even after this corrupt media onslaught, nine out of ten Americans remained firmly anti-war—until the sinking of the *Lusitania*. This tragedy was the direct consequence of a policy introduced by another famous Freemason who would later lead his nation through World War II. His name was Winston Churchill.

During World War I, Churchill was first lord of the admiralty and he was very keen for America to join. In 1914, he issued an order which changed the British naval rules of engagement. Previously, gentlemanly conduct demanded that a warship be given the chance to escape, rather than being ambushed or blasted out of the water. Churchill ordered his merchant ships to ignore such a warning if they were confronted, for instance, by a surfacing U-boat, and even to counter-attack. This forced German U-boats to launch torpedoes underwater, with the inevitable consequence that, in Churchill's own words, they "ran the greater risk of mistaking neutral for British ships and of drowning neutral crews and thus embroiling Germany with the other Great Powers."

The following year just such an accident occurred when the *Lusitania* was torpedoed by a German U-boat on May 7, 1915 and nearly 1,200 people, including over a hundred Americans, drowned. There are many who believe that the liner was deliberately placed in danger, and that it was packed with ammunition to guarantee that it would sink with spectacular certainty.

According to the British commander Joseph Kenworthy, who was on board, the ship's military escort was withdrawn and the captain was ordered to slow down, when it was well known that there was a U-boat operating in the area. According to Colin Simpson, "The Germans, whose torpedo struck the liner, were the unwitting accomplices, or victims of a plot . . . concocted by Winston Churchill."

However, despite the best efforts of Churchill, it was the notorious Zimmermann Telegram which was the final straw. It was an intercepted telegram from German foreign secretary Arthur Zimmermann to the German ambassador in Mexico, promising to help Mexico regain lost territory in Texas, Arizona and New Mexico, in return for Mexico's support if the United States entered the war. Marrs sums up its incongruity: "no one will ever know why something so audacious was produced or why it was acknowledged once discovered." However, the results are plain for all to see: "Tremendous amounts of debt were created, while only those who collected the interest benefited. As always, it was the American public that suffered the real losses in dead relatives, devalued money, and enduring foreign commitments."

MONEY MATTERS: BIRTH OF BANKING, DOLLAR BILL, AND THE EURO

"Money—whether a piece of paper or a figure on a computer screen—is intrinsically worthless, yet it fuels the modern world. The trappings of money and banking have been compared to those of a religion, yet only those who profit from it understand the inner workings of the money cult. And they work hard to keep it that way."

—*Jim Marrs,* Rule by Secrecy

BIRTH OF BANKING

The Knights Templar, who had close links with Freemasonry, were responsible for the birth of banking. According to Baigent and Leigh "they pioneered the concept of credit facilities, as well as the allocation of credit for commercial development and expansion. They performed, in fact, virtually all the functions of a twentieth century merchant bank." At the peak of their power "the Templars handled much, if not most, of the available capital in Western Europe."

Travelers in Europe and the Holy Land faced many hazards and did not want to carry large sums of money around. So the Templars developed a system whereby a pilgrim could deposit money at a Templar temple in his home country in return for a special coded receipt (the equivalent of the modern traveler's check) which could be cashed in at any temple along the route.

Baigent and Leigh also point out that in England the Templars acted as tax collectors: "Not only did they collect papal taxes, tithes and donations, they collected taxes and revenues for the crown as well—and seemed to have been even more fearsome in that capacity than [Britain's] Inland Revenue . . . In 1294, they organized the conversion of old to new money. They frequently acted as trustees of funds or property placed in their custody, as brokers and as debt collectors. They mediated in disputes involving ransom payments, dowries, pensions and a multitude of other transactions."

Right: Gualdim Paei, Grand Master of Knights Templar, 1160 A.D.

Jim Marrs compares them to the "medieval equivalent of today's multinational corporation" since "along with banking practices, the Templars brought to Europe their acquired knowledge of architecture, astronomy, mathematics, medicine, and medical techniques" and that "granted the privilege to build their own churches, the Templars became the prime movers behind the construction of the great medieval cathedrals of Europe." There can be no doubt that the interests of the Templars were inextricably bound up with the medieval masons.

THE DOLLAR BILL

Based on the proposition that at least one (Ben Franklin) and possibly two (Thomas Jefferson) of the men who created the first design for the Great Seal in 1776 were Freemasons, certain design details on the one dollar bill have been highlighted by numerous commentators as proof that Masonic symbolism is imbedded in the economic make-up of the most powerful country in the world.

These details, and the theories which are attached to them, range from the plausible to the absurd, but all are included here, to show the depth of feeling that this issue has raised over the years.

ALL-SEEING EYE

The detail cited most often is the logo of a pyramid with an eye positioned at the top, which some conspiracy theorists see as proof alone that the world's bankers are being led by the Illuminati and Freemasons. Its significance has already been discussed on page 40: how it was a familiar artistic convention, representing the omniscient "Ubiquitous Deity," and how it wasn't limited to Masonic circles. This "Eye of Horus" was symbol of ancient Egyptian religion and has been appropriated by many other groups as the "evil eye" and the all seeing "eye of god."

The triangle is an isosceles, made up of two right angle triangles with sides of five, twelve, and thirteen units, which illustrates the 47th Problem of Euclid (also known as Pythagoras's Theorem: that in a right-angled triangle the square of the hypotenuse—the longest side—is equal to the sum of the squares of the other two sides).

EAGLE

In 1955, the Grand Lodge of Texas published the following insights regarding Masonic symbolism in the design of the dollar bill:

"On the obverse is an eagle whose dexter wing has thirty-two feathers, the number of ordinary degrees in Scottish Rite Freemasonry. The sinister wing has thirty-three feathers, the additional feather corresponding to the 33rd degree of the same Rite conferred for outstanding Masonic service. The tail feathers number nine, the number of degrees in the Chapter, Council, and Commandery of the York Rite of Freemasonry."

The lodge also points out that the total number of feathers is sixty-five "which, by gematria, is the value of the Hebrew phrase YAM YAWCHOD (together in unity)." This phrase is taken from Psalm 133 and is apparently used in the first degree ritual.

GOAT-HEAD PENTAGRAM

The demonic "Goathead" pentagram, which some believe has been deliberately included in the street layout of Washington, D.C. (*see page 161*), can also be made to appear on the great seal by joining certain letters to spell the word "Mason" in the inscriptions "*Annuit Cæptis*" and "*Novus Ordo Seclorum.*" Draw a line from the M of *Seclorum* to the A of *Annuit* to the O of *Ordo* to the S of *Cæptis* to the N of *Novus.*

Some sources believe that the words "Novus Ordo Seclorum" (suggested by Charles Thomson for the final design for the reverse side of the Great Seal in June 1782) means "New World Order." It doesn't. It is taken from Virgil's "Eclogue IV," a pastoral poem that expresses the longing of the world for a new era of peace.

PAGAN OWL

A miniscule pagan owl is said to be hiding in the upper right corner of the side which shows George Washington. It can be found at the top left of the detailed frame which surrounds the number "1." (The owl has long been associated with occult practices and the search for esoteric knowledge.)

THE EURO

On January 1, 2002, twelve European countries delivered up their financial sovereignty and adopted the single European currency, the EURO, while conspiracy theorists railed that European enlargement and the European Central Bank were a major leap forward in the Illuminati-Masonic plan to introduce a one-world government.

However, whereas the Masonic symbolism on the U.S. dollar bill is incorporated into the design, with the EURO it is the design. Each of the seven EURO notes pays homage to the founding principle of Freemasonry—architecture. These images represent the seven architectural styles that have marked European culture: Classical, Romanesque, Gothic, Renaissance, Baroque and Rococo, iron and glass architecture, and modern architecture.

However, the introduction of the EURO is far more serious than loss of sovereignty, it is the fact that it ushers in a new age of financial transactions—it was the first electronic currency. It existed for three years purely as an e-currency before the notes came into circulation. If coming off the gold standard was phase one of the Illuminati-Masonic financial master plan, then phase two is the EURO, which critics say is a stepping stone to the elimination of hard currency (coins and notes) in favor of smart cards and cashless transactions. Our governments tell us that we will benefit from fraud protection and ease of use, but this cleverly disguises the attack on our civil liberties. When financial transactions are electronic, governments can control how we spend our money.

Richard Poynder, the chairman of the Smart Card Club, which encourages the use of electronic money, is on record as saying: "Special software could actually prevent recipients of social security benefits from squandering their money on 'banned products and services such as alcohol or gambling.' We could ensure they don't spend money on the 'wrong' things . . . A young man trying to spend his dole money in a bar would find his card refused by the central computer."

If placing Masonic symbols on the U.S. currency was daring, the design and implementation of the EURO was nothing short of a blatant advertisement.

P2 Lodge and the Vatican Bank

Of all the concerns regarding Masonic involvement in world affairs, one of the most intriguing, though under-reported (at least in the U.S.), is that of the P2 "*Propaganda Due*" Masonic lodge and the murder of Roberto Calvi.

Nicknamed God's banker because of his links with the Vatican, Calvi was found hanging under Blackfriars Bridge in London in 1982. He was chairman of the Vatican-controlled Banco Ambrosiano, Italy's largest private bank, who had fled to Britain from Italy after it had collapsed owing $1.3 billion and he was facing arrest for the illegal export of currency and suspected fraud and money laundering. At the time a London inquest jury ruled that he had committed suicide, but this decision was overruled in 1983 and replaced by an open verdict. Recently, the case has been reopened and four men face possible trial for his murder. Many sources connect this scandal not only to the P2 lodge but also with the CIA and high-ranking American Masons.

The *Propaganda Due* lodge was founded in Rome in 1877. Jim Marrs describes how in the 1980s a man named Licio Gelli turned this "little-used Italian Masonic lodge into what was termed a 'worldwide fascist conspiracy' with the help of the Mafia, the Vatican Bank and the CIA." Gelli became a Mason in 1963, and by 1966 had gained control over P2 and increased its membership to nearly one thousand. Marrs continues, "Obviously, Gelli had help. Italian journalist Mino Pecorelli, a P2 member himself, claimed the CIA was funding P2, a charge echoed by CIA contract agent Richard Brenneke in 1990." David Icke claims that the P2 lodge was also connected to "the Carbonari, an amalgamation of Freemasons, the Mafia and the [Italian] military."

According to Marrs, a P2 plot to "fabricate so much leftist terrorism that the Italians would demand an authoritarian or even fascist government" was discovered by Italian authorities in 1981 along with "a list of the Masonic conspirators' names, which included three cabinet ministers, forty members of Parliament, forty-three military generals, eight admirals, security service chiefs, the police chiefs of four major cities," and a host of other diplomats and civil servants. He also reports that P2 were implicated in several acts of terrorism, including the 1980 Bologna train bombing, the 1988 bombing of Pan Am Flight 103 over Lockerbie, and the murder of Italian Prime Minister Aldo Moro

in 1978, but the story, while reported in the London *Independent* newspaper, received "scant attention in the American media, even when it grew to implicate top Vatican officials, American bishop Paul Marcinkus and [Henry] Kissinger."

Many people feel that Calvi's death was symbolically Masonic. The noose around his neck calls to mind the cabletow that is placed around a candidate's neck during the Entered Apprentice ceremony (*see page 187*). He died "where the tide ebbs and flows," recalling the first degree oath (*see page 187*), although his throat was not cut, nor his tongue removed. The bricks that filled his pockets may represent the rough ashlar (*see page 47*) that "represents man in his infant or primitive state," or inevitably they could have been used to weight him down.

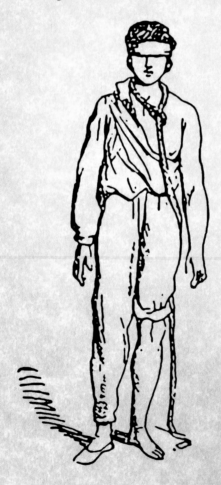

According to Martin Short, "Calvi was one of many P2 members to die a strange death. In 1979 Mino Pecorelli, a journalist, was shot dead through the mouth after publishing damaging information about Gelli's perfidious past. In 1986, Michele Sindona died after allegedly poisoning himself with a cup of coffee laced with potassium cyanide. He had just started a life sentence for murder."

The Vatican's role in the Banco Ambrosiano scandal has been used as evidence that Pope John Paul I was murdered for attempting to root out financial and Masonic corruption in the Holy See. "The Vatican Bank" is the name given to the Institute for the Works of Religion (IOR). It is personally owned by the Pope and loans money to religious projects worldwide. However, it became involved with risky speculations with Banco Ambrosiano during the 1970s, when it began to take advantage of its status as an off-shore bank.

Banco Ambrosiano began as a special "Catholic bank" for the Church in Milan; when the IOR bought shares in Ambrosiano, Calvi loaned and laundered money through it. However, even after he had been convicted of currency fraud in 1981, the IOR continued to deal with him and, according to journalist Sandra Miesel, "it even gave him 'letters of comfort' saying that the IOR controlled Calvi's Panamanian shell corporations in exchange for Calvi's promise that it would not be liable for their debts." When Calvi's fraud was uncovered, an arrest warrant was issued for the President of the IOR, Archbishop Paul Marcinkus, whom Pope John Paul I had attempted to remove from office for corruption three years earlier, but he stayed inside the Vatican City, immune to prosecution, until charges were eventually dropped.

The Mystery of Rosslyn Chapel

The most famous and mysterious of Masonic buildings is a small chapel built in the fifteenth century in a small old mining village south of Edinburgh, Scotland. Rosslyn Chapel is thought by many historians to be hiding as many secrets as the Egyptian pyramids, not least the mystery surrounding the highly ornate "Prentice Pillar" in the south of the chapel.

According to legend, the master mason, who should have done the carving, traveled to Rome to research its proposed design. While he was away, one of his apprentices had a vivid dream in which the design of the pillar was revealed to him, and he realized his vision in his master's absence. When the master mason returned, he was so incensed and jealous of the exquisite craftsmanship of the pillar that he killed the apprentice by striking him with his hammer. This story has been seized upon by the authors of *The Hiram Key*, which pointed out the parallel with the murder of Hiram Abiff (*see page 15*). Furthermore, they suggest that a stone head carved in the chapel depicting a man with a gash on his forehead is further proof that the Masonic ritual murder actually took place.

Rosslyn is one of the most ornately-carved fifteenth-century medieval stone chapels in Europe. It was commissioned and designed by Sir William St. Clair, who became the first Scottish Grand Master. The elaborate symbolism carved into its interior has particular relevance to Freemasonry, and several Templar knights are buried beneath the chapel, leading many to speculate that it is the final resting place of the Holy Grail. The famous grail-seeker Trevor Ravenscroft claimed in 1962 that the grail was actually hidden inside the Prentice Pillar. Metal detectors have proved that there is indeed a metal object buried inside the pillar, but the current Lord Roslin refuses to allow the pillar to be X-rayed. Other grail-seekers believe that the Templars hid secret scrolls from Solomon's Temple in the chapel's subterranean vaults which reveal the true identity of Christ.

ALBERT PIKE, THE KU KLUX KLAN, AND THE NEW WORLD ORDER

It is impossible to research the history of Freemasonry without coming across the name Albert Pike. He was one of the most famous Masonic dignitaries of the nineteenth century and wrote several Masonic works, including *Morals and Dogma of the Ancient and Accepted Scottish Rite of Freemasonry*. This is one of the most widely read occult books in the world, and it is still presented to Masons who have reached the 32nd degree.

ALBERT PIKE

Albert Pike was born on December 29, 1809, in Boston, and was the oldest of six children. He studied at Harvard, and later served as a Brigadier-General in the Confederate Army. After the Civil War, like many Confederate leaders, he was found guilty of treason and jailed. However, he was well-connected—fellow Freemason President Andrew Johnson pardoned him on August 30, 1865. He later became a 33rd Degree Mason. He is the only Confederate leader with a statue on federal property in Washington, D.C. It stands near the foot of Capitol Hill, between the Department of Labor building and the Municipal Building, and attempts by Lyndon H. LaRouche during the 1992 presidential campaign to have it removed drew fierce opposition from the Masonic community.

Some people have claimed that Albert Pike is to Masonry what Shakespeare is to literature, while certain Masonic sources try to distance themselves from him altogether, claiming he was a man of his age. He was a top leader in the Knights of the Ku Klux Klan, and others accuse him of being a Satanist and Grand Master of a Luciferian group known as the Order of the Palladium (or Sovereign Council of Wisdom), supposedly founded in Paris in 1737 and introduced into the inner circle of Masonry.

But his most sinister legacy is that he may have established a blueprint for a New World Order which involved three world wars and one world government, which some people believe is being carried out today in the upper ranks of Freemasonry.

THE KU KLUX KLAN

The Ku Klux Klan's rise to power sprang out of the resentment of many white Southerners and Confederates after the Civil War. It was formed in the winter of 1865 by six young Confederate veterans in the small town of Pulaski, Tennessee, and some sources claim it was initially nothing more than a drinking club and that the first night rides were irresponsible and childish pranks. This may be true, but these rides quickly got out of hand, and blacks became the primary targets of threats and violence. Within three years this secret organization had spread to neighboring states, hijacked by powerful leaders such as General Nathan Bedford Forrest, a Confederate cavalry officer and the Klan's first Imperial Wizard, and Albert Pike, who held the office of Chief Justice of the Ku Klux Klan while he was simultaneously Sovereign Grand Commander of the Scottish Rite, Southern Jurisdiction. He wrote the anthem and the rules of the organization.

Pike's racism is well documented. He expressed his vision of Masonic brotherhood in an editorial on April 16, 1868 of the Memphis, Tennessee, *Daily Appeal*, which he owned and published:

"With negroes for witnesses and jurors, the administration of justice becomes a blasphemous mockery . . . We would unite every white man in the South, who is opposed to negro suffrage, into one great Order of Southern Brotherhood, with an organization complete, active, vigorous, in which a few should execute the concentrated will of all, and whose very existence should be concealed from all but its members."

And in a letter in 1875 he wrote of Freemasonry: "I took my obligation to White men, not to Negroes. When I have to accept Negroes as brothers or leave Masonry, I shall leave it."

Albert Pike also wrote many articles about the mythical super-race of the Aryans, praising their virtues, imagined history, and religion which he tried to show was the precursor of Freemasonry.

THE NEW WORLD ORDER

Albert Pike is believed to have had close links with Italian revolutionary Giusseppe Mazzini, who was a 33rd degree Mason who became head of the Illuminati in 1834 and whom some credit with founding the Mafia in the 1860s.

Conspiracy theorists claim that Pike aimed to bring together Mazzini and two other 33rd degree Masons—Lord Henry Palmerston of England and Otto von Bismarck of Germany—to use the Palladian Rite to create an occult umbrella group that would unite all Masonic groups.

These same sources claim that Pike wrote a letter to Mazzini, dated August 15, 1871, in which he outlined his vision for three world wars which would ultimately bring about one world government. There is no trace of the original letter today, which is reputed to have been on display at the British Museum in London for a short time.

Pike's Illuminati plan was as simple as it has proved effective. It called for Communism, Nazism, political Zionism, and other international movements to be organized and used to foment three global world wars and at least two major revolutions. The following are extracts from the letter, showing how three World Wars have been planned for many generations.

"The First World War must be brought about in order to permit the Illuminati to overthrow the power of the Czars in Russia and of making that country a fortress of atheistic Communism. The divergences caused by the 'agentur' (agents) of the Illuminati between the British and Germanic Empires will be used to foment this war. At the end of the war, Communism will be built and used in order to destroy the other governments and in order to weaken the religions."

"The Second World War must be fomented by taking advantage of the differences between the Fascists and the political Zionists. This war must

be brought about so that Germany is destroyed and that the political Zionism be strong enough to institute a sovereign state of Israel in Palestine. During the Second World War, International Communism must become strong enough in order to balance Christendom, which would be then restrained and held in check until the time when we would need it for the final social cataclysm."

"The Third World War must be fomented by taking advantage of the differences caused by the 'agentur' of the "Illuminati" between the political Zionists and the leaders of Islamic World. The war must be conducted in such a way that Islam (the Moslem Arabic World) and political Zionism (the State of Israel) mutually destroy each other . . . We shall unleash the nihilists and the atheists and we shall provoke a great social cataclysm which in all its horror will show clearly to all nations the effect of absolute atheism; the origins of savagery and of most bloody turmoil. Then everywhere, the people will be forced to defend themselves against the world minority of the world revolutionaries and will exterminate those destroyers of civilization and the multitudes disillusioned with Christianity whose spirits will be from that moment without direction and leadership and anxious for an ideal, but without knowledge where to send its adoration, will receive the true light through the universal manifestation of the pure doctrine of Lucifer brought finally out into public view. A manifestation which will result from a general reactionary movement which will follow the destruction of Christianity and Atheism; both conquered and exterminated at the same time."

Above: Big Three Conferees Posing for Portrait —Prime Minister Clement Attlee of Great Britain; President Harry S. Truman; and Marshal Josef Stalin of Russia

MASONIC INFLUENCES IN WASHINGTON, D.C.

The extent of Masonic power today is unclear, but close scrutiny of the street map of Washington, D.C. quickly reveals their influence in the nineteenth century. In *The Temple and the Lodge*, Michael Baigent and Richard Leigh declare "the Capitol and the White House were each to become focal points of an elaborate geometry governing the layout of the nation's capital city. This geometry, originally devised by an architect named Pierre-Charles l'Enfant, was subsequently modified by Washington and Jefferson so as to produce specifically octagonal patterns incorporating the particular cross used as a device by Masonic Templars."

They don't expand upon this idea, but there is no shortage of commentators who claim that Freemasons hid their two most important occult symbols, the pentagram (five-pointed star) and the "Square and Compass," at the heart of the U.S. governmental administration.

Drawing a straight line from the White House to Scott Circle, to Washington Circle and on to Mt. Vernon Square, Dupont Circle and back to the White House, the most potent pentagram in the occult symbolic repertoire—the demonic "Goathead"—becomes chillingly apparent. According to occult experts, its four upper points represent the elements of Fire, Water, Earth, and Air, and the bottom point, The White House, the mind of Lucifer. The more extreme anti-Masonic commentators insist that this pattern is intended to demonstrate that the White House would be ruled by Satanic Freemasons.

This same site forms the upper tip of a Masonic compass, one arm of which runs along Pennsylvania Avenue to the Capitol, which is at the top of the compass. The second arms follows Maryland Avenue and ends at the Jefferson Memorial.

Futhermore, according to J. Edward Decker "The center of the pentagram is 16th St. where, thirteen blocks due north of the very center of the White House, the Masonic House of The Temple sits at the top of this occult iceberg." He continues, "Every key federal building from the White House to the Capitol Building has had a cornerstone laid in a Masonic ritual and had specific Masonic paraphernalia placed in each one."

OBELISKS AND OSIRIS

The Washington Monument, which lies directly west of the Capitol, is an obelisk—a tall, four-sided stone pillar tapering toward a pyramidal top. Some people believe that this is the most significant occult symbol of all. Most people are aware that an obelisk is Egyptian in origin, but few know the story behind it, and fewer still that it is an important Masonic symbol. In fact, the four obelisks which sit in four major Western cities—Paris, London, New York, and Washington, D.C.—were erected specifically because of the efforts of, and large sums of money donated by, prominent and powerful nineteenth-century Freemasons.

In ancient Egypt the obelisk, known as a "benben" stone, was a symbol dedicated to the sun god, Ra, the creator of humanity and the source of all life. The Egyptians believed that they channeled the spirit of Ra during certain times of the year, and were an important feature in ritualistic human sacrifice. The pharaohs of later dynasties continued this tradition of obelisk building, but they dedicated theirs to Osiris, God of the earth, the Underworld, and life after death. The Osiris myth contains a powerful message of reincarnation, since his son Horus resurrected him using a "lion grip." In the third degree of Freemasonry, the candidate is raised using a lion grip. The connection between Freemasonry and ancient Egyptian gods cannot be more explicit than at this moment. Osiris is an important figure for the Freemasons. As Martin Short points out in *Inside the Brotherhood*, "If, as some Masonic historians claim, Hiram Abiff is really Osiris reborn, there could be no greater proof of Masonic ascendancy in the modern world than Egyptian obelisks thrust by Masons into the heart of the West's greatest cities."

An obelisk was erected in the Place de la Concorde in Paris in 1833 under the supervision of the Minister of Public Works, Louis Thiers, a Freemason. The London obelisk, now known as Cleopatra's Needle, was, like the French obelisk, a gift from the Viceroy of Egypt, Mohammed Ali, in 1819. But it wasn't transported from Egypt until 1877, when an eminent Mason, general Sir James Alexander shipped it to London, with financing by another Mason, Dr. Erasmus Wilson, at a cost of £20,000. In the same year, its twin was given to America and once again it was Masons who organized and financed the transportation from Egypt. According to Martin Short, "The prime mover was a New York editor named William Hulbert, the benefactor (to the tune of $75,000) was William J. Vanderbilt, and the sailor was a Lt-Cmdr Henry Gorringe. All were Freemasons." To confirm its importance to Freemasonry, the erection of the cornerstone in Central Park in 1880 "was a brazenly Masonic affair," says Short. "Nine thousand Freemasons marched with bands through the streets to Greywacke Knoll where Jesse Anthony, the Grand Master of New York Masons, laid the 7-ton cornerstone." Finally, when the Washington Monument was completed, Short describes the dedication ceremony which took place in February 1885 as "another dose of fraternal self-congratulation. One prominent brother spoke of Masons now as builders of human society."

Left: The Washington Monument

Prominent nineteenth-century 33rd Degree Mason Albert Mackey admits in *A Manual of the Lodge* that Masons worship the Sun as God, in common with pagans throughout history, but he doesn't stop there. He makes the connection between the obelisk (point within a circle) and the phallic worship of Osiris: "The point within the circle is an interesting and important symbol in Freemasonry . . . The symbol is really a beautiful but somewhat abstruse allusion to the old Sun-Worship, and introduces us for the first time to that modification of it, known among the ancients as the worship of the phallus."

It is difficult to ignore the signposts which Masons have left to one of their greatest open secrets, not hidden within the lodge, but on public display in major cities and in the writings of Masonic authors who commanded respect among their Masonic peers: Freemasonry has at its center the symbols and signs of a pagan fertility cult.

SIRIUS AND VIRGO

In *The Secret Architecture of Our Nation's Capitol*, astrologer David Ovason maintains that twenty complete zodiacs have been placed in the capital, "each one pointing to an extraordinary mystery" and "oriented in a meaningful way." He believes that the layout of Washington, D.C. was aligned with the stars and dedicated to the Dog Star, Sirius, which many hold as the occult designation of Satan. (Sirius is sacred to the god, Set, the evil Egyptian god who killed Osiris. It is also known as the Eastern Star.)

His premise is that architect Pierre-Charles L'Enfant aligned Pennsylvania Avenue so that each year, on August 10, it would be possible to stand at the Capitol building and look down the avenue to see the setting sun. At this moment the sun is in 17 degrees of Leo and the star Regalus sets over the White House just over half an hour after sunset, leaving the star Spica in Virgo, and Arcturus in Bootes. According to Ovason "they are the three stars which Masons such as Pike and Brunet recognized as enclosing the constellation of Virgo." He concludes that "the city was intended to celebrate the mystery of Virgo—of the Egyptian Isis, the Grecian Ceres and the Christian Virgin."

He also suggests that Spica may have been the origin of the Blazing (or Flaming) Star of Freemasonry." Later he says that Spica, is really Sirius, "represented in hieroglyphics that resembled an obelisk and a five-pointed star."

Ovason also asserts that the cornerstones of various buildings were laid on specific days after consulting astrology. For example, he says, "in the arch of skies on the day the foundation stone for the White House was laid, there was a most interesting conjunction. Shortly before noon, the Moon had entered the same degree as the Dragon's Head (a node of the Moon). Both planet and node were in 23 degrees of Virgo . . . time and time again, as we study the Masonic involvement in the building of this city, through almost two centuries, we shall see emphasis placed on this sign Virgo. Time and time again, we shall see that a knowledge of the stars played an important part in every stage of the creative phases in the construction of the city."

Right: Engraving Of Constellation Virgo

Epilogue

This book has demonstrated that the Freemasons, far from being a spent force, have during the last few decades been active in financial, political, religious, and criminal circles, influencing world events and bringing their goal of one-world government ever closer. Some denounce nineteenth-century Masonic aficionados such as Albert Pike as being on the extreme fringes of Masonry, but today, as then, the Masonic agenda continues to exert its malign influence in many areas of our lives.

In 1913 Woodrow Wilson said, "Some of the biggest men in the United States, in the field of commerce and manufacture, are afraid of something. They know that there is a power somewhere so organized, so subtle, so watchful, so interlocked, so complete, so pervasive, that they better not speak above their breath when they speak in condemnation of it."

Little has changed since then. The Blue Lodge Masons continue to pay their dues and meet in the spirit of brotherly camaraderie while the upper echelons press forward with their Hegelian schemes.

Today, Masonry exists in 164 countries, with six million members, and there are nearly 34,000 lodges worldwide. While Masonic membership may have dwindled, anyone who believes that Masonry is in decline is gravely mistaken.

Right: Freemason of Grande Loge Nationale Francaise, a Lodge based in Paris, France

An initiation ceremony at a Masonic Lodge in France

Appendix (i)

The Degrees of the Rite of Perfection (with the Corresponding Degrees of the Ancient and Accepted Scottish Rite Shown in Brackets)

Symbolic Degrees

1. Apprentice [Entered Apprentice]
2. Companion [Fellow Craft]
3. Master [Master Mason]

Ineffable Degrees

4. Secret Master
5. Perfect Master
6. Intimate Secretary
7. Provost and Judge [Intendant of the Buildings]
8. Intendant of the Buildings [Provost and Judge]
9. Master Elect of Nine
10. Master Elect of Fifteen [Illustrious Master Elect of Fifteen]
11. Illustrious Elect Chief of the Twelve Tribes [Sublime Knight Elected]
12. Grand Master Architect
13. Knight of the Royal Arch [Royal Arch of Enoch]
14. Grand Elect, Ancient Perfect Master [Grand Scottish Knight of the Sacred Vault (of James VI) or Sublime Mason]

HISTORICAL DEGREES

15. Knight of the East, or of the Sword
16. Prince of Jerusalem

PHILOSOPHICAL DEGREES

17. Knight of the East and West
18. Knight of the Rose-Croix [Sovereign Prince of Rose-Croix]

TRADITIONAL AND CHIVALRIC DEGREES

19. Grand Pontiff or Master ad Vitam [Grand Pontiff or Sublime Scotch Mason]
20. Grand Patriarch Noachite [Venerable Grand Master of Symbolic Lodges]
21. Grand Master of the Key of Masonry [Noachite or Prussian Chevalier]
22. Prince of Libanus
23. Chief of the Tabernacle
24. Prince of The Tabernacle
25. Knight of the Brazen Serpent
26. Prince of Mercy
27. Sovereign Commander of the Temple
28. Knight of the Sun
29. Grand Scottish Knight of St. Andrew
30. Grand Elect Kadosh
31. Grand Inquisitor Commander
32. Sublime Knight Commander of The Royal Secret
33. Grand Inspector-General

A Brief Summary of the Degrees

Here is a summary of the teachings of each degree. There is insufficient space to detail all the props, symbols, and lighting in each case; this is intended to give an overview of each degree. The rituals of the first three degrees are examined in detail in the next chapter.

1° Entered Apprentice

This degree is the beginning of a man's journey into Freemasonry. It represents youth.

2° Fellow Craft

This degree is symbolic of adulthood and represents labor.

3° Master Mason

This degree represents the wisdom of old age.

4° Secret Master

This degree teaches the importance of fidelity and integrity. After the death of Hiram, Solomon selects seven of the most worthy and skilled Master Masons and appoints them special guardians of the Sanctum Sanctorum of the temple. They are called the Secret Masters. The number seven is important as it relates to the seven cardinal virtues, the seven ages of life, the seven laws of Noah, and the seven days of the week.

The Lodge represents the Sanctum Sanctorum and is hung in black and strewed with white tears as the lodge is in mourning for Hiram. The seven-branch candlestick burns in the east and provides the only light in the lodge. Over the east is hung a circle (a serpent with its tail in its mouth) enclosing three interlaced triangles to form nine beams of light and a blazing star in the center. In the center of the star is a 9, and where the triangles overlap are the characters E, A, J, J, Y, A, O, A, H, the initials of the nine sacred words.

5° PERFECT MASTER

This degree teaches the destructive nature of unworthy ambitions and the importance of duty to family, country, and God. Respect is paid to the departed brother. The lodge is hung with green cloth from eight white columns. Hiram's coffin is in front of the altar, which is draped in black. Marks of blood are placed in the northeast section of the lodge, and the star in the interlaced triangle of the Secret Master's degree now shines red.

6° INTIMATE SECRETARY

This degree teaches the importance of respecting the secrets of others. It relates to an incident in King Solomon's Audience Chamber where a spy had been eavesdropping. Solomon pardons him. It also teaches that a trustworthy person can survive false accusations. The lodge represents the audience-chamber of King Solomon's Temple. It is hung with black, strewed with silver tears, and has twenty-seven lights in three groups of nine toward the east, west, and south.

7° PROVOST AND JUDGE

This degree teaches the importance of compassionate justice and relates to the appointment of judges to resolve disputes among workmen during the building of the temple after Hiram's death. The lodge represents the middle chamber of the temple. It is hung with red, and in the east is hung a blue canopy, embellished with stars. It is lit with five lights.

8° INTENDANT OF THE BUILDINGS

This degree teaches the pursuit of truth and wisdom over and above personal title and status. It relates to the appointment by Solomon of five Superintendents. The lodge represents the middle chamber and is hung with crimson, with a blue canopy in the east. There are twenty-seven lights, in three groups of nine.

9° MASTER ELECT OF NINE

This degree teaches that Truth emerges from the clash of opinions and that a man should not be led away by overbearing zeal. Also, it teaches the overthrow of ignorance by freedom. The lodge is hung with black, and there are nine great lights.

10° MASTER ELECT OF FIFTEEN

This degree teaches about fighting for the cause of the oppressed against the oppressor and of toleration against intolerance; that is, to the cause of human freedom, corporal and mental, against tyranny exercised over the soul or body. Ambition and fanaticism that enslave us will be overthrown by the sword of justice and freedom. The lodge is hung in black, strewn with red and white tears. There are fifteen lights.

11° SUBLIME KNIGHT ELECTED

This degree teaches that the true and faithful Brother who is brave and loyal and pursues what is right with honesty and sincerity, will be rewarded. The lodge is hung in black and strewn with red and white tears. There are twelve lights in threes forming an equilateral triangle.

12° GRAND MASTER ARCHITECT

This degree teaches that consistency of purpose and the exercise of Mercy through compassion enables us to overlook one's injuries and the shortcomings of others and the wrongs against us. The lodge is hung with white with crimson flames. There are three great lights: one in the east, one in the west, and one in the south.

13° KNIGHT OF THE ROYAL ARCH

This degree enacts the story of Enoch to whom God appeared in a vision as a pure golden triangle, and said, " Enoch, thou hast longed to know my true name: arise and follow me, and thou shalt know it." It prepares the Brother for the next degree and the climax and conclusion of the Ineffable degrees.

14° GRAND ELECT MASON

In this degree the lodge represents the Secret Vault under the Sanctum Sanctorum. It reveals and explains the tetragrammaton (the four Hebrew letters usually transliterated as YHWH or JHVH, used as a name for God), and narrates the completion of the temple and its eventual destruction and the death of Solomon.

15° KNIGHT OF THE EAST, OR OF THE SWORD

This degree recounts the Babylonish captivity, which lasted seventy years, the return of 42,360 captives to Jerusalem and the subsequent attempt to build a second temple, under the command of Zerubbabel, which took forty-six years to construct. The Masons were instructed to work with a sword in one hand and a trowel in the other. It teaches the need to be alert, to be ready for work or combat, and the importance of perseverance, conviction, and devotion to Truth.

16° PRINCE OF JERUSALEM

The story follows on from the preceding degree and represents the hardships endured by the Masons as they rebuild the temple. They are rewarded for their perseverance by completion of the second temple in the sixth year of the reign of King Cyrus. It marks the end of the Historical Degrees.

17° KNIGHT OF THE EAST AND WEST

The first of the Philosophic Degrees, it teaches that one should learn from one's mistakes to avoid repeating the errors of one's ancestors. When the Knights and Princes united to conquer the Holy Land, they vowed to spend the last drop of their blood to establish the true religion of the Most High God. After peace was made they could not fulfill their vows, so they resolved to do in theory what they could not do in practice.

18° KNIGHT OF THE ROSE-CROIX

This degree reaffirms the need for tolerance of other beliefs and religions. The Israelite, the Moslem, and the Christian may stand side by side, and hand in hand, as brethren. Masons must seek to free the mind of all encumbrances in the quest to contemplate immutable truth and to attain the knowledge of the divine.

19° GRAND PONTIFF

This degree is founded upon certain apocalyptic mysteries relating to the New Jerusalem; it rests upon the three characteristic virtues taught in the eighteenth degree, and proclaims the Alpha and Omega. It concerns itself with the eternal struggle between darkness and light, good and evil, and examines how to overcome the errors and frailties of humanity. The first mention is made of Universal Religion.

20° GRAND PATRIARCH NOACHITE

This degree examines the duties, powers, and privileges of a Master and the Masonic principles and leadership are designated and related to Masonic intelligence attained, through patient labor and the study of Masonic law and the symbolic legends of the Order.

21° GRAND MASTER OF THE KEY OF MASONRY

This degree teaches that Freemasonry should shield and protect the innocent from unjust accusation, but it does not conceal, justify, or condone wrongdoing of its brethren. The knot of Masonic alliance is broken by an overtly guilty or evil act.

22° PRINCE OF LIBANUS

In this degree, the honor of honest labor is demonstrated and the need to improve the condition of those who toil and who seek to improve civilization, the advancement of humankind, and the destruction of barbarism and ignorance.

23° CHIEF OF THE TABERNACLE

This degree teaches that those with strong faith will make great sacrifices in order to help their fellow man. The form of the Tabernacle is described, along with the old sacerdotal ceremonies of the ancient temples.

24° PRINCE OF THE TABERNACLE

This degree emphasizes the power of faith, the universality of faith, the immortality of the soul, and the importance of cultivating and strengthening the spirit rather than pleasure seeking.

25° KNIGHT OF THE BRAZEN SERPENT

This degree relates to the time when the Israelites were pitched in the desert on the eastern side of the mountains of Hor, Seir, or Edom after the death of Aaron. It teaches that faith must sustain us through the inevitable wilderness years in every person's life.

26° PRINCE OF MERCY

The Christian Masons met in the Catacombs during the persecution under Domitian, the emperor of Rome. This degree calls to mind the meetings, in private places, of the faithful who were bound by a solemn promise not to disclose or even converse about the secrets of the mysteries.

27° SOVEREIGN COMMANDER OF THE TEMPLE

The Knights guard the city of Jerusalem against the Saracens to protect the feeble and oppressed, and to defend the innocent. They displayed the five qualities of humility, temperance, chastity, generosity, and honor, and they practiced all the Masonic virtues.

28° Knight of the Sun

This degree teaches that the interplay of opposites is vital for the whole and is the key of all the secrets of nature. Harmony and equilibrium exist through the interplay of opposites. The absolute is reason, which exists through itself and does not depend on a corollary.

29° Grand Scottish Knight of St. Andrew

This degree emphasizes the Masonic requisites of equality and toleration. God is unknowable in his entirety; therefore, no one Church or religion expresses the unity of the Divine. We must, therefore, respect the beliefs of others, because nobody has access to the whole of His light.

30° Grand Elect Kadosh

This degree sets out how the Knight Kadosh must arm himself with Faith and Love in order to defend the Order and help the weak and injured with humility, fidelity, and prudence.

31° Grand Inquisitor Commander

This degree teaches that to render judgment is a stern duty; to do so a man must be just and upright. Every man should be given the benefit of innocence and purity of intentions and be forgiven if there is hope of reformation.

32° Sublime Knight Commander of the Royal Secret

The Knights Kadosh are the legitimate successors of the Templars. This degree describes the victory of the spiritual over the human, of reason over excess. Philanthropy is a practical reality. No virtue is acquired in an instant, but step-by-step.

33° GRAND INSPECTOR-GENERAL

This is how the Latin Constitutions of 1786 describe this degree:

"The 33rd degree confers on those Freemasons who are legitimately invested with it, the quality, title, privilege, and authority of Sovereign, Supremorum, Grand Inspectors-General of the Order. The peculiar duty of their mission is to teach and enlighten the Brethren; to preserve charity, union, and fraternal love among them; to maintain regularity in the works of each Degree, and to take care that it is preserved by others; to cause the dogmas, doctrines, institutes, constitutions, statutes, and regulations of the Order to be reverently regarded, and to preserve and defend them on every occasion; and, finally, everywhere to occupy themselves in works of peace and mercy."

The 33rd and last degree is awarded to Scottish Rite Freemasons who have shown outstanding service to their Order and the community. You cannot apply for this degree but must be recommended by several high-ranking 33rd degree Freemasons.

Freemason's Hall in London, England in 1808

Appendix (ii)

INITIATION RITES

If Masonry is known for one thing, it is the observation of, from the perspective of a non-Mason, bizarre, childish, sinister, and impenetrable rituals. Without a little knowledge of what underpins them, it is impossible to decipher their meaning, relevance, and even dignity.

The Masons' primary teaching method is ritual. They take place behind closed doors with a guard (called a Tyler) standing outside the lodge room. Masons are also issued with little books called "monitors," which are published by the Grand Lodges. They contain explanations of major symbols and rituals. Critics of Masonry believe these monitors teach a path of salvation that does not depend on Jesus Christ, and they highlight the baptism of the third degree as evidence of this, since the initiate is instructed to imitate Hiram Abiff if he wishes to enter the celestial lodge above where the Grand Architect of the Universe (the Masonic god) presides.

The lessons and teachings in each degree are different, but the mechanics of all the rituals are very similar. The candidate must change his clothes and be blindfolded. He is guided into a lodge room, kneels at an altar, his blindfold is removed, and he is taught special signs, grips (handshakes), and passwords. He is presented with the corresponding tools of that degree, is led out of the lodge room to change back into his clothes, and then receives further instruction in a lecture.

Masonry denies that it is a religion. However, the initiation ceremonies of the first, second, and third degrees are tantamount to a baptism and rebirth. Initiates are being baptized into the religion of Freemasonry. Much like a stage hypnotist might make a subject perform acts he otherwise might not do, some believe that the Masonic rituals use peer pressure and the fear tactics usually associated with fraternities, to hoodwink initiates. Extensive use of the allegory and symbolism means that a committed Christian will find himself joining a new religion. Masonic critics maintain that it takes a strong person, especially one who is in the company of his father or, perhaps, grandfather or friends, to put a stop to the proceedings and say that he feels uncomfortable.

Stephen Knight, in *The Brotherhood*, claims that during ritual ceremonies for the Holy Royal Arch exaltation, candidates learn the lost name or word of God, said to be "Jahbulon." Knight maintains that most Masons do not realize the significance of the name, which he defines as a combination of three names: *Jah*, for the Hebrew god Yahweh; *Bul*, the ancient Canaanite fertility god Baal and devil; and *On*, for Osiris, the Egyptian god of the underworld.

There now follows a condensed summary of the key elements of initiation ceremonies for each degree.

Right: A parade of African American Masons in New Orleans

ENTERED APPRENTICE DEGREE

The Worshipful Master calls the meeting to order and makes sure that all present are Masons. The meeting is opened at the Entered Apprentice Degree. Brother Tyler (the guard) keeps guard outside the door to "observe the approach of cowans and eavesdroppers, and suffer none to pass or repass."

A candidate is prepared for the first degree of freemasonry by having all metal items removed from his person; he must be "neither naked nor clothed, barefoot not shod, left knee and breast bare, hood-winked [blindfolded], and with a cable-tow [noose] about his neck." He enters the lodge blindfolded after knocking three times. As soon as he enters, the Senior Deacon stops him by pressing the compass against his naked left breast, to signify the pain and torture he will receive should he ever reveal Masonic secrets.

He is directed to the center of the lodge where the Worshipful Master leads a prayer over him. He is then led to the east for his examination by the Worshipful Master. He must do this in "due and ancient form" by forming a square by taking a step with his left foot and then placing the heel of his right foot in the hollow of the left. He advances to the sacred altar of freemasonry, where he kneels on his left knee (which is naked), with his right forming the angle of a square, his left hand supporting and his right resting on the Holy Bible, square, and compasses.

He then swears an oath of allegiance, never to reveal Masonic secrets, including the words, "to all of which I do solemnly and sincerely promise and swear, without any hesitation, mental reservation, or secret evasion of mind in me whatsoever; binding myself under no less a penalty than that of having my throat cut across, my tongue torn out, and with my body buried in the sands of the sea at low-water mark, where the tide ebbs and flows twice in twenty-four hours, should I ever knowingly or wilfully violate this, my solemn Obligation of an Entered Apprentice." He kisses the Bible, and the noose is removed from his neck, whereupon he is asked what he most desires, to which he replies, "Light in Masonry."

Next, the candidate is shown the Masonic grip (handshake), known as "Boaz" (*see page 57*). The Worshipful Master then presents the candidate with his lambskin (white leather apron). He is told it is "an emblem of innocence and the distinguished badge of a Mason." He is instructed that no matter what greatness he may achieve in his life, that "never again from mortal hands . . . shall any honor so distinguished, so emblematical of purity and all perfections" be conferred upon him as the honor of receiving the Masonic apron.

The Worshipful Master requests a metallic substance from the candidate, which of course he cannot provide, as all metal objects have been removed from his person. He is instructed that should he meet another human being, especially a brother Mason in any "like destitute situation," he should "contribute to his relief as liberally as his necessities might require, and [his] ability permits."

The candidate, now clothed in his apron, is presented with the working tools of the Entered Apprentice, which are the 24-inch gauge and the common gavel.

The Entered Apprentice now receives a lecture explaining the symbolism contained within the ritual he has just taken part in. The reason why all metallic substances were removed is because at the building of King Solomon's Temple, "there was not heard the sound of an axe, hammer, or any metal tool," because all the measuring, shaping, and fitting was done in the quarry or forest with such precision, that when the parts were assembled, they fitted perfectly and "it resembled more the handiwork of the Supreme Architect of the Universe than that of human hands."

He was neither naked nor clothed, because Masonry disregards material wealth and worldly honors. Being neither barefoot not shod relates to an ancient Israelite custom mentioned in the Book of Ruth, of a man of taking off his shoe and giving it to his neighbor as testimony of the sincerity of his intentions.

The candidate is blindfolded so that he may perceive with his heart before his eye, and to symbolize that he is in darkness and that once he has received the light of Masonry he should keep others in the dark with regards to Masonic secrets. Had he not conformed to the ceremony, he would have been led out of the lodge by means of the noose.

He kneels on his left naked knee, the weaker side, to teach that he is taking on the weaker part of Masonry, that of Entered Apprentice (the bottom of the hierarchy).

The lecture ends with further moral instructions and the Entered Apprentice is told that before he can become a Fellow Craft he must commit a certain lecture to memory. The Worshipful Master closes the lodge.

FELLOW CRAFT DEGREE

The Worshipful Master calls the meeting to order and makes sure that all present are Fellow Crafts. Brother Tyler (the guard) is instructed that the Worshipful Master is about to open a lodge of Fellow Crafts. The Tyler keeps guard outside the door to "observe the approach of cowans and eavesdroppers, and suffer none to pass or repass."

A candidate is prepared for the second degree of freemasonry by having all metal items removed from his person; he must be "neither naked nor clothed, barefoot not shod" as before, only this time he bares his right knee and right breast. He is hood-winked [blindfolded] but the cable-tow [noose] is wound twice around his right arm.

He enters the lodge after knocking three times. He states that of his own free will he seeks "More Light in Masonry." The Senior Steward gives the password, "shibboleth," on his behalf. This time the square is pressed to his right naked breast, to teach him that "the square of virtue should be a rule and guide" for his practice through life. He is led around the lodge, and the password is given several times. He travels with the Senior Deacon from the west to the east of the lodge, in search of more light in Masonry. The Worshipful Master directs them to the Senior Warden in the west, who teaches the brother how to approach the east in "due and ancient form."

He forms a square by taking a step with his left foot and then taking an additional step with his right foot, placing the heel of his left foot in the hollow of the right. (This is known as the "dueguard," which a Fellow Craft must use as a sign of respect to the Worshipful Master and also when entering or leaving a Fellow Crafts lodge.) He advances to the sacred altar of Freemasonry, where he kneels on his right knee (which is naked), with his left forming the angle of a square, his left hand in a vertical position, his right hand resting on the Holy Bible, square and compasses.

Right: Freemason Major R. Lawrence lays the foundation stone at a hospital in Brighton, England

He then swears an oath of allegiance never to reveal Masonic secrets, including the words, "to all of which I do solemnly and sincerely promise and swear, without any hesitation, mental reservation, or secret evasion of mind in me whatsoever; binding myself under no less a penalty than that of having my left breast torn open, my heart and vitals taken thence, and with my body given as a prey to the vultures of the air, should I ever knowingly or wilfully violate this, my solemn Obligation of an Fellow Craft." He kisses the Bible and the noose is removed from his arm, whereupon he is asked what he most desires, to which he replies, "More Light in Masonry."

Next the candidate is shown the Masonic pass-grip (handshake) known as "Shibboleth" and the real grip of a Fellow Craft known as "Jachin." The candidate is shown how to wear his apron in the manner of a Fellow Craft, that is, with the flap turned down at the lower left corner, and tucked up in a triangle form a pocket.

He is presented with the working tools of the Fellow Craft that are the plumb, square, and level. The plumb encourages him to walk upright, the square to be virtuous, and the level is a symbol of mortality and the passage of time.

The Fellow Craft now receives a lecture that is "principally devoted to the explanation of physical science." The first mention is made of ancient operative Grand Master Hiram Abiff, the Chief Architect of the building of King Solomon's Temple. Abiff is the central character in the third degree ritual. Symbolism of winding stairs is introduced, a journey between that the two pillars erected at the entrance to the porch of King Solomon's Temple. The name of these pillars are "Boaz" (representing strength) to the left and "Jachin" (representing establishment) to the right.

The candidate then gains access to the Middle Chamber of King Solomon's Temple after using his newly learned passwords and grips. Here, his attention is drawn to the letter "G" suspended in the east, and its importance as the initial letter of "geometry," the basis of freemasonry, and its greater meaning as the initial of God.

The lecture ends with further moral instructions, and the Fellow Craft truth is told that before he can become a Master Mason, he must commit a certain lecture to memory.

The Worshipful Master closes the lodge.

MASTER MASONS DEGREE

The Worshipful Master calls the meeting to order and makes sure that all present are Master Masons. Brother Tyler (the guard) is instructed that the Worshipful Master is about to open a lodge of Master Masons. The Tyler keeps guard outside the door to "observe the approach of cowans and eavesdroppers, and suffer none to pass or repass."

A candidate is prepared for the third degree of freemasonry by having all metal items removed from his person; he must be "neither naked nor clothed." He is barefoot, has both knees and breasts bare, is hoodwinked [blindfolded], and has the cable-tow [noose]wound three times around his body.

Appendix(1)

ROOSEVELT THE MASTER MASON

He enters the lodge after knocking three times. This time he states that of his own free will he seeks to be raised to the Sublime Degree of Master Masonry. The Senior Steward gives the password "Tubalcain" on his behalf. This time, the points of the compass are pressed to his right and left breast simultaneously, to teach him and that the vital organs are contained within the breast and symbolically that the most valuable tenets of Freemasonry are held within the points of the compass, which are friendship, morality, and brotherly love.

He is led around the lodge and the password is given several times. He travels with the Senior Deacon from the west to the east of the lodge, in search of more light in Masonry. The Worshipful Master directs them to the Senior Warden in the west, who teaches the brother how to approach the east in "due and ancient form." He advances on his left foot as an Entered Apprentice would, then on his right as a Fellow Craft, then takes an additional step on his left, bringing his two heels together to form the angle of a square. (This is known as the "dueguard," which a Master Mason must use as a sign of respect to the Worshipful Master and also when entering or leaving a Master Mason's lodge.)

He then swears an oath of allegiance, never to reveal Master Mason secrets, including the words, "to all of which I do solemnly and sincerely promise and swear, without any hesitation, mental reservation, or secret evasion of mind in me whatsoever; binding myself under no less a penalty than that of having my body burned to ashes, on the ashes thereof scattered to the four winds of heaven, that there might remain neither track, trace nor remembrance among man or Masons of so vile and perjured a wretch as I should be should I ever knowingly or wilfully violate this, my solemn Obligation of a Master Mason." He kisses the Bible, and the noose is removed from his body, since, as the Worshipful Master points out, "we now hold this Brother by a stronger tie." He is asked what he most desires, to which he replies, "More Light in Masonry."

Next, the Master Mason is shown the Master Mason pass-grip (handshake) known as "Tubalcain" and the real grip of a Master Mason. The candidate is shown how to wear his apron in the manner of a Master Mason, turned down to form a square, the perfect figure that symbolizes the integrity of his service to God and reminds him of his four duties: to country, neighbor, family, and himself.

Left: Master Mason Theodore Roosevelt

He is presented with the working tools of the Master Mason, which are all the working tools of Masonry including the trowel, which symbolically spreads the cement of brotherly love, which binds Masons together.

When a Freemason is initiated into the third degree he must be struck on the forehead in the dark and knocked backwards into a coffin. He is then lifted up by his Master Masons and confronted with the real human skull of a Mason who broke his vows of secrecy.

The candidate plays the part of Hiram Abiff, the Grand Architect at the building of King Solomon's Temple, who is unjustly killed, buried, and then raised from the grave. Hiram had new secrets that enabled him to pass himself off as a Master Mason. Upon completion of the temple, the workers had been promised that those who were faithful would be told the secrets, but three of the Fellow Crafts decided to export the secrets from Hiram. Their names are Jubela, Jubelo, and Jubelum. When Hiram refused they killed him. The candidate now undergoes the first part of his symbolic baptism-death. At midnight he is buried. Usually, this involves being placed in an open coffin; however each lodge develops the details of a ritual to suit itself. So it is reasonable to assume that some watchers may go as far as actually burying a candidate and shoveling earth on top of the coffin.

Right: Freemasons' Annual General Meeting in 1992

The three Fellow Crafts are executed at the command of King Solomon, played by if the Worshipful Master. Twelve Master Masons, playing the part of a Fellow Crafts, recant their murderous designs and present themselves before King Solomon, wearing white gloves and aprons (symbolic of their innocence) and confess and beg his pardon. A search begins to find the remains of Hiram Abiff. The body is dug up again, and Solomon declares that he will devise a secret word that will be used as a substitute until the real word, the secret word which died with Hiram, has been found again.

The Senior Grand Warden attends to raise the body using the grip of an Entered Apprentice. Because the body is badly decayed, this fails. So he applies the grip of a Fellow Craft, which also fails. Finally, the Worshipful Master uses the grip of a Master Mason to successfully raise the body. Significantly, the body is raised "from a dead level to a living perpendicular."

As the candidate is raised, he and the Worshipful Master adopt the position known as the "five points of fellowship," which is foot to foot, knee to knee, breast to breast, hand to back, and cheek to cheek (or mouth to ear). The Worshipful Master whispers the words "Mah-Ha-Bone" into the candidate's ear (derived from "Macbenae," which means "The flesh falls from the bone." Another interpretation is "What! The Builder"). This is the substitute secret word. The candidate has experienced resurrection. He is then shown the real grip or lion's paw of a Master Mason.

Finally, the nine classes of Masonic emblems are delineated: the pot of incense, the beehive, the book of constitutions, which is guarded by the Tyler's sword, the sword pointing to the naked heart, the anchor and the Ark, the forty-seventh problem of Euclid, the hourglass, and the scythe.

The Worshipful Master closes the lodge.

Right: 8,000 Freemasons attending lunch at Olympia in London, England

Recommended Reading

THE TEMPLE AND THE LODGE
Michael Baigent and Richard Leigh, Arcade
Publishing, 1991

SYMBOLS OF FREEMASONRY
Daniel Beresniak, Barnes & Noble Books, 2003

EARLY HISTORY AND ANTIQUITIES OF FREEMASONRY
Joseph F. Ford, Kessinger Publishing, 1998

THE LOST KEYS OF FREEMASONRY
Manly P. Hall and J. Augustus Knapp, Philosophical Research
Society Inc, 1996

THE SIGN AND THE SEAL: THE QUEST FOR THE LOST ARK OF THE COVENANT
Graham Hancock, Touchstone, 1993

JACK THE RIPPER: THE FINAL SOLUTION

Stephen Knight, Bounty Books, 2000

RULE BY SECRECY: THE HIDDEN HISTORY THAT CONNECTS THE TRILATERAL COMMISSION, THE FREEMASONS AND THE GREAT PYRAMIDS

Jim Marrs, Harper Paperbacks, 2001

THE FREEMASONS: A HISTORY OF THE WORLD'S MOST POWERFUL SECRET SOCIETY

Jasper Ridley, Arcade Publishing, 2002

BORN IN BLOOD: THE LOST SECRETS OF FREEMASONRY

John J. Robinson, M. Evans and Company Inc, 1990

SHOULD A CHRISTIAN BE A MASON

E.M. Storms, Impact Christian Books, 1999

Index

Index

Index

Photo and Illustration Credits